BIRMINGHAM FOOD

A MAGIC CITY MENU

EMILY BROWN

AMERICAN PALATE

Published by American Palate
A Division of The History Press
Charleston, SC 29403
www.historypress.net

Front cover, top right: Photograph of Frank Stitt. *By Arik Sokol.*
Back cover, inset: Photograph of Carole Griffin. *By Arik Sokol.*

First published 2015

Manufactured in the United States

ISBN 978.1.62619.807.4

Library of Congress Control Number: 2015941001

Notice: The information in this book is true and complete to the best of our knowledge. It is offered without guarantee on the part of the author or The History Press. The author and The History Press disclaim all liability in connection with the use of this book.

For my dad, who gave me his appetite, and my mom,
who taught me to appreciate a good story.

CONTENTS

ACKNOWLEDGEMENTS

If writing this book has taught me anything, it's that community is the biggest part of what makes Birmingham special, and this book would not have been possible without my community. First off, I'd like to thank Jen Barnett, who gave me my first real start in food writing and steered The History Press in my direction when it approached her about a book on Birmingham food. I'd also like to thank James Little and REV Birmingham for allowing me to cheerlead for my favorite chefs and restaurateurs for Birmingham Restaurant Week and giving me the space to try new restaurants and hear new stories, all in the name of Birmingham enthusiasm. A special thank-you is due to the Southern Foodways Alliance and its interview transcripts from many Birmingham restaurateurs who have passed on. The work the alliance does to preserve the food-related cultural history of the South is inspiring and impressive. Thanks also to Charles and Carrie Beth Buchanan, Joy and Dusty Johnston and Jill Marlar for your encouragement and support. My friends are the best. Danielle Derise and Robin Mozer generously gave their time and expertise during early drafts, keeping me on track and well spoken. Without Arik Sokol's talent, shown in some of the photographs in these pages, this book wouldn't be half what it is, and I couldn't have found someone more fun with whom to pal around and photograph chefs. And thanks to George Atkinson for your help editing these amazing images. My family has been my foundation for everything I do, and this book has been no exception. My mom and my grandmother have both been incredible sounding boards. Mostly I'd like to thank James Brown, my husband, for his eternal positivity, willingness to share any sort of foodie adventure, patience with my times of stress and steadfast belief in me. Plus, he gave me some pretty adorable babies. (You are.)

INTRODUCTION

Everybody knows that southerners are, by nature, full of hospitality. And Birmingham has a legitimate claim to that birthright of good manners, good service and good food. Since the beginning of the twentieth century, many of Birmingham's favorite restaurants have been owned and run by families, with some businesses spanning three or more generations. The pride taken in these family establishments extends beyond the food and into the dining rooms, where the prevailing atmosphere implies diners are guests at the family table, there to be taken care of whether in casual or high style.

From our early history of hotel and cafeteria dining—coffee and steaks served with a smile—to the Greek immigrants who brought a dedication to quality ingredients and their own cultural spin on traditional southern fare, service and hospitality have always been at the forefront of Birmingham dining. With families running the front and back of house and sons learning the business from their fathers, it's no wonder diners stay loyal to restaurants where they're remembered by name and sometimes by their drink orders. These days even Highlands Bar and Grill, arguably one of the best high-end restaurants in the country, is just as famous for how it makes customers feel when they walk in the door as it is for its Baked Grits and other culinary creations from Chef Frank Stitt.

Birmingham's restaurant scene is known for its Greek restaurateurs, many of whom emigrated from the same region in Greece. One of these is George Sarris, whose Fish Market restaurant downtown has been in business in some form since the 1960s and is now run with the help of his son Dino. Greek families run meat-and-three cafeterias with soul food served alongside Greek chicken and fish. They've run hot dog stands that served block-long lines daily, and they've even become known for barbecue at places like Jim 'N Nick's. Diners in the Magic City can find some truly tasty Greek food from a variety of establishments, and they look forward to the annual Greek Festival in September as much for the chocolate baklava as the rice pilaf.

Barbecue in Birmingham can spark lively debate. Whether the sweet and thick tomato-based sauce at Golden Rule, the vinegary sauce from Ollie's of the past or the tangy white sauce covering smoked chicken at Saw's suits your tastes, everybody has a favorite and an opinion. Birmingham boasts a long history of barbecued meats, but the future is looking beyond the usual presentations and traditional cuts of pork, beef and chicken to inventive options like sliders with Asian flair from one food truck and unusual cooking methods like ash at Chris Hastings' new casual spot. These days our hot dogs, served at local pubs and food stands, are getting an upgrade to house-made sausages and even veggie dogs with radical toppings.

The biggest change the history of Birmingham restaurants has seen, without a doubt, was the opening of Highlands Bar and Grill in 1982. Chef Frank Stitt brought the philosophy of local, seasonal ingredients prepared simply and with great care to his restaurant and to Birmingham at the forefront of a national movement just beginning to sprout. The quality of Chef Stitt's food and his mentorship of other chefs in his kitchens spread his influence to the wide variety of restaurants across the city that have created national buzz about Birmingham dining. The current community of restaurants in Birmingham has him to thank for coming into its own as a culinary destination. Birmingham has grown into a modern city that thrives on its foodie culture, boasts multiple James Beard Award–winning chefs and provides some of the most welcoming places to sit down and have a memorable meal, from a neighborhood gastropub to a white tablecloth establishment focused on hospitality as an art form.

As a Birmingham native, I've been privileged to eat at many of the restaurants detailed in these pages over the years, as well as many great ones that are not—either because they've gone or simply because a second, or even third, volume would be necessary to manage them all. We southerners really do know our food. My apologies go to those not mentioned by name. And as the revitalization of downtown brings more and better dining options to the city's main corridor and beyond, the question when going out to eat is always how to narrow down your options.

INTRODUCTION

We're a city with a troubled past but a bright future. Enthusiasm and energy are spreading throughout the city as makers and doers create everything from craft beer and craft cocktails to business and recreation districts that are bringing our downtown back to life. Robust and simple dishes, prepared from the best ingredients, fuel these developments in which there's room for everyone at the table, those with traditional and new ideas alike. Food in Birmingham has been on the upswing for a while now, quietly building a reputation for more than just fried chicken and turnip greens. This is a story of memories, of family, of values passed down like secret recipes; sometimes the qualities handed down are intangible, but the result on the plate is always tasty.

I can only hope that I am uniquely qualified to tell these stories because they're in my blood. My great-grandmother ran a small restaurant—the Market Café—with her Greek husband. It was located on First Avenue across from the farmers' market and Niki's, and it supported my grandmother and her brother throughout childhood when they would ride the streetcar into downtown Birmingham to go to the movies and most definitely to eat some of our famous hot dogs from places like Tom's Coney's. My grandmother, if you can convince her, still makes a mean baklava. I've been talking to chefs and restaurateurs for years now through my work with Freshfully, a now closed grocery store specializing in local food, and Birmingham Restaurant Week, and I'm always humbled by how nice these people are and how willing they are to share their passion to create beautiful and satisfying food. They sense that their restaurant kitchens and dining rooms are just an extension of their own lives and homes because these establishments are their lives. They work with family, they are husband-and-wife teams, they are sons and daughters taking over the family business and they spend all their time—all of it—pouring out their love for food and quality ingredients for us, the customers. This book is my thank-you for that love and sacrifice and a letter for the city that wants everyone to taste how wonderful it can be.

1
EARLY DINING

Formed near the farming town of Elyton in the Jones Valley basin in 1871 as a mining and steel production town, Birmingham has always been part of the "New South," the term for the changed South after the Civil War. The industrial growth and subsequent need for workers made Birmingham a booming town in the early 1900s, full of immigrants who would later become important in establishing the city's restaurant and dining scene. With a population that ballooned from 38,415 in 1900 to 178,806 in 1920—with anywhere from 2 to 5 percent of those being foreign born—Birmingham, in its founding years, was on course to be one of the biggest metropolitan cities in the South.

Aside from mining great deposits of iron ore, coal and limestone, leading to a robust industry in steel production, young Birmingham was also a city of businessmen inhabiting the new skyscrapers popping up all over downtown. Real estate made many rich, though banking, finance and retail were also lucrative professions. These busy men were part of a new class of southerner, aristocratic due to industry rather than by virtue of owning land and running plantations, as in days past. And these prosperous businessmen, unlike the previous inhabitants of the farming towns where Birmingham now stood, needed sustenance and diversion.

As a general rule, dining out at the turn of the twentieth century was not something most southerners were interested in. Larger port cities like Savannah and Charleston had some reputable restaurants, but when traveling and thus forced to eat away from home, southerners could expect to encounter terrible food at hotels and roadside taverns. Accounts from that time depict a grim scene: dirty tables, greasy food and questionable skills in management. Larger cities like Birmingham were more likely to have nicer hotels where better and more reliable food was served, especially as the practice of dining out became more popular.

A menu from January 12, 1902, from the Hotel Hillman shows gourmet, if limited, dining options for Birmingham residents and travelers. With oyster cocktail for starters, along with "Baked Trout au Gratin" and "Boiled Blue Fish" as entrée options, it's easy to see that Birmingham's relative proximity to the coast encouraged seafood choices, even at such an early stage. "Boiled Ox Tongue with New Spinach," "Braised Sweetbreads aux Champignons" and "Paupiettes of Veal Auxelles" for additional entrée choices demonstrate that the fascination with all things French began early in Birmingham, as well as the idea that "French" was a signifier of upper class, though one has to wonder if the fancy names of dishes were masking less than exceptional quality given refrigeration and transportation technology at the time. Several varieties of potatoes or peas were available to accompany the entrées, which also included roast beef, turkey and lamb. But dessert showed the most interesting range of choices, with anything from "Pine Apple Pudding à la Richilleu" to peach or mince pie, "Jelly au Maraschino" or ice cream and "Assorted Cake[s]" available. Coffee and tea were the only beverage accompaniments listed.

The southern diet of the time still relied heavily on farm produce, milk and meat for those people in or close to rural areas, and in newer cities like Birmingham, restaurants and cafés served food similar to what people were used to eating at home. More reputable restaurants in the Carolinas and Atlanta served plentiful spreads, available for under a dollar and sometimes under fifty cents, including regional delicacies such as country sausage, ham sandwiches, spareribs, hominy, turnips, collard greens, sweet potatoes, black-eyed peas, okra, tomatoes, cornbread, biscuits, honey, pecan pie, tea and coffee—all of which you can still find at quality meat-and-threes like Ted's or Niki's today, though for an appropriately higher price. Water was the most popular drink, but coffee and tea were also thoroughly enjoyed. Many people even roasted and ground their own beans for their morning coffee. After purchasing beans from the store, people would roast them to the desired darkness in the oven and then grind them in hand-cranked grinders. Alabamians reportedly preferred a darker roast and finer grind. Tea in the early twentieth century was enjoyed hot until the advent of icehouses, and then electric refrigerators in the 1920s and '30s made cooling the drink practical and easier. Adding lemon and sugar to the icy beverage created sweet tea, the drink most synonymous with southern refreshment.

A brief look at the *Birmingham Age-Herald* from 1905 reveals no restaurant reviews, though plenty of ads for liquor and its curative powers can be found sprinkled among the ads for suits and stores. One advertisement from November invites readers to a benefit dinner "for the support of bed in Charity Ward" for the sweet price of fifty cents. Dinner, at that time, was served from 12:00 to 3:00 p.m. Another advertisement for the new Red Cross Pharmacy drugstore makes mention of its soda fountain and "the best seasonable drinks," so maybe inhabitants of young Birmingham appreciated the farm-to-table movement long before its invention. Aside from these casual meals, hotel dining was still the place for a nice dinner in Birmingham.

Tutwiler Hotel

The Tutwiler Hotel, built in 1914 on Fifth Avenue North, became one such establishment, boasting visitors as famous as President Warren G. Harding and notorious actress Talullah Bankhead, known for her party-girl antics as much as her dusky-voiced screen presence. Notable Birmingham businessman Robert Jemison built the hotel to try to persuade the Alabama Iron and Steel Institute to hold its yearly convention there. Since the owner of the Tutwiler Coal, Coke and Iron Company, Major Edward M. Tutwiler, provided financing, he was awarded the honor of being the hotel's namesake. With a ballroom big enough to hold a banquet, party or meeting for 1,200 people, the Tutwiler established itself as one of the city's premier hotels. Guests in the Tutwiler's early years could avail themselves of one of the hotel's 343 rooms for just $1.50, but double rooms with a bath were extra.

A postcard advertising the hotel's grand ballroom and banquet hall illustrates the beauty of the original design. Large white columns lined the outside of the room's wide wooden floor and supported a beautiful balcony and white wooden railing, from which guests could view the festivities going on below. Delicate yet large crystal chandeliers hung from the ceiling in multiple places. Another postcard, this time for the main dining room on the first mezzanine, shows full, silky drapes covering the large arched windows and elegant white walls dense with architectural detail.

An early menu from the Tutwiler's Continental Dining Room shows quite the variety of gourmet options for diners to choose from. Highlights

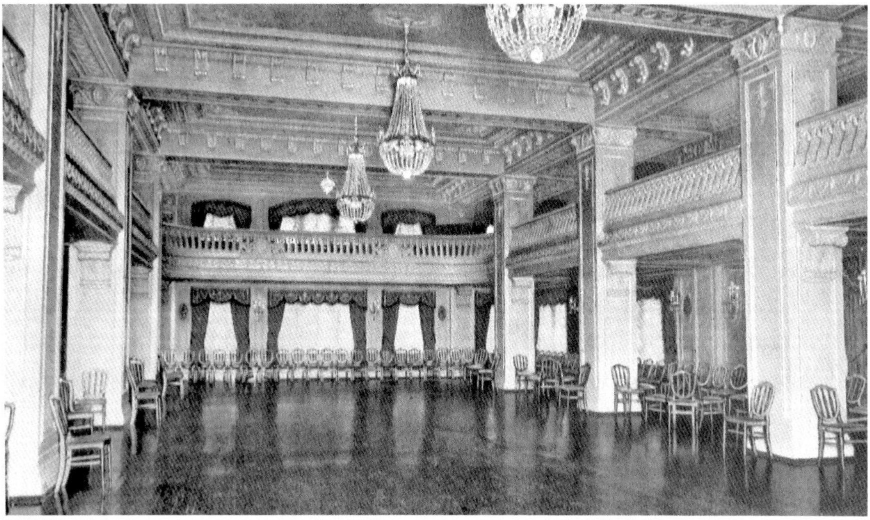

Postcard image of the Tutwiler Hotel banquet hall. *Courtesy of Steve Gilmer and What's on Second; photograph by Emily Brown.*

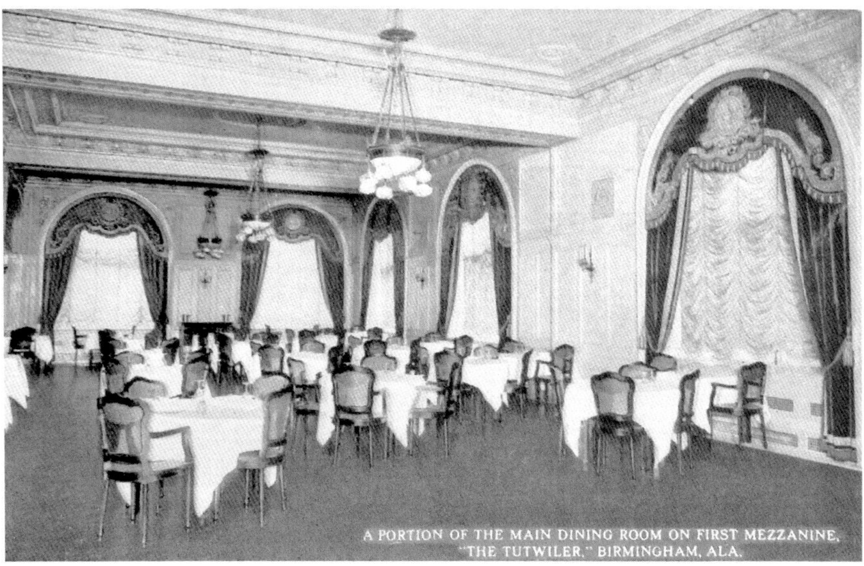

Postcard image of the Tutwiler Hotel dining hall located on the first mezzanine. *Courtesy of Steve Gilmer and What's on Second; photograph by Emily Brown.*

include Blue Point oysters for $0.75 a half dozen; "Clear Green Turtle Soup with Sherry" for just $0.60; an extensive listing of broiled, grilled and fried seafood "From the Sea Coast"; broiled steak, lamb, pork and chicken; and "Tutwiler Specialties," such as "Grilled or Sauted [*sic*] Calf's Liver with Rasher Bacon" for $1.50 and "Tennessee Ham Steak, Red Gravy" for $2.10. Vegetable and salad options were all à la carte as well, though the tastes of the time are clearly reflected by the few varieties of both. Both broccoli and asparagus were served with hollandaise sauce, and a whopping eight potato dishes are listed. For salads, diners could enjoy a simple "Hearts of Lettuce" for $0.40, an elegant half avocado for $0.60 (filled with chicken or shrimp salad for $1.25) or several varieties of Chef's, Waldorf or potato salad, all served with bread and butter and complimentary French or Thousand Island dressing. Roquefort Cheese Dressing would run patrons an additional $0.25. In the Continental Room at the Tutwiler, sandwiches ranging from chicken salad and club to salami and even a hamburger were also served. Or patrons could enjoy "Assorted Cheeses" like Swiss, American, Liederkranz and Camembert before desserts such as the "Green Apple Pie .25, with Cheese .35," "Compote of Fruit," "Sherbet" or even "Peach Melba." In the beverage department, milk and buttermilk were offered by the bottle, and coffee, tea and chocolate were offered by the pot.

Sadly, the Tutwiler's condition declined as the hotel's ownership changed hands, and in 1972, it closed for good. Two years later, the hotel was imploded to make way for construction of a new bank, a fact that still saddens many Birmingham residents. In 1986, the Tutwiler got a second chance at life, through the former Ridgley Apartments, also constructed by Robert Jemison and owned by the Tutwiler family. The apartments, located on Twenty-first Street around the corner from the original location, were renovated and reopened as the new Tutwiler Hotel.

Currently a member of the Hampton Inn family of hotels, the Tutwiler still has a home for fine dining under its roof. Open for lunch and dinner, as well as special events, Century Restaurant and Bar serves locally sourced food prepared in gourmet southern style. Anything from French onion soup to grilled fish from the Gulf can grace the tables at Century, where diners can soak up the historic atmosphere while enjoying their meal.

In addition to hotel dining for travelers or those of means, places for workingmen and women to grab a quick lunch or linger over coffee while discussing the news of the day were available in downtown Birmingham and increasing with the city's growing population of industrial workers and businessmen. The key to increased demand for restaurants in the early days of dining was businessmen. Gentlemen of the era were free to frequent restaurants where activities like drinking and smoking took place alongside dining. Ladies, however, were considered to have more delicate sensibilities, to be prone to offense or injury in proximity to this type of inappropriate behavior and, therefore, to be in need of protection, so they were often relegated to eating at home or in "Ladies' Cafés" on the rare occasion they needed sustenance while shopping or running errands downtown. Even lunchrooms, such as the Albert Café, offered special seating for white women when they couldn't offer an entirely separate dining room or restaurant. Women were invited to sit "at the tables," presumably to help insulate them from too close contact with unfamiliar men.

As dating became a more popular activity starting in the 1920s, co-ed dining options became more commonplace, and men would often take their wives out to dinner for a "night off." Here is where large ballrooms like that at the Tutwiler or beautiful surroundings like the murals and tile work showcased at the Bright Star in nearby Bessemer gained popularity. As the immigrants who'd flooded into the city began to find success in the restaurant industry, opening cafés and seafood restaurants around Birmingham in particular, more options for those nights out became available, increasing the popularity of dining as a form of entertainment. Birmingham citizens took great pride in their status as part of a modern, cosmopolitan city that supported so much new business. The newspaper even boasted about the city's ranking over other southern cities. Residents embraced the moniker "Magic City"—given by one of the city's founders, Colonel James R. Powell, because of the city's fast-paced growth from relative wilderness.

Britling Cafeteria

Starting in 1919, a new style of restaurant opened in Birmingham: the cafeteria. Britling Cafeteria was supposedly one of the first cafeterias in the South. A man named A.W.B. Johnson opened a Britling on First Avenue and soon expanded to two other locations, one on Third Avenue and one on Twentieth Street; the latter two were connected through the kitchen, though diners had to enter each location separately. With his fast success, Mr. Johnson soon sold the franchises to the Holcomb family, and they ran and expanded the business for the next fifty years. Britling Cafeterias quickly became popular among the city's residents, as they offered inexpensive meals served in a modestly elegant atmosphere. Women who needed a quick bite while running household errands downtown could safely stop in to dine, families could enjoy a hearty meal on the town to give mothers a break from cooking and couples could linger over coffee after enjoying a matinee nearby.

Postcards advertising various Britling locations showcase the pristine dining rooms with white tablecloths covering intimate tables. At one time, the First Avenue Britling Cafeteria decoration took advantage of springtime floral colors, with bouquets lining the half walls that separated tables and large arrangements in vases set on the bar and against the walls. The steam table at another location featured prominently in the center of the restaurant, its silver top gleaming as much as the highly polished floors and sparkling racks of glassware that sat at the ready for serving water or tea. The first Britling Cafeteria closed its doors in 1964, when its building was sold, and the other downtown locations didn't last much longer. But suburban locations continued to serve diners into the early 1980s. Current Birmingham diners looking downtown for a quality meal served quickly, for which Britlings were known, have more options than they've had since those last Britling Cafeterias closed. Tau Poco, Urban Standard, Brick and Tin, Trattoria Centrale and others have taken up the mantle of what is now called fast casual dining in Birmingham.

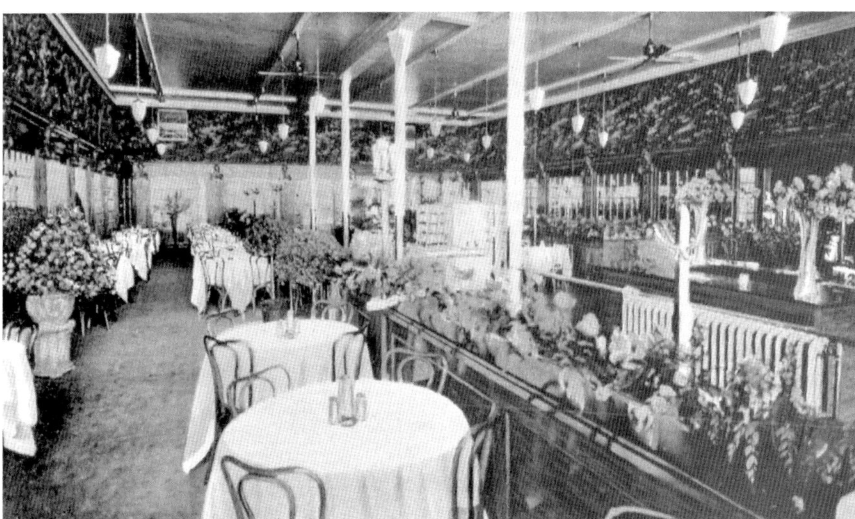

Postcard image of Britling Cafeteria. *Courtesy of Steve Gilmer and What's on Second; photograph by Emily Brown.*

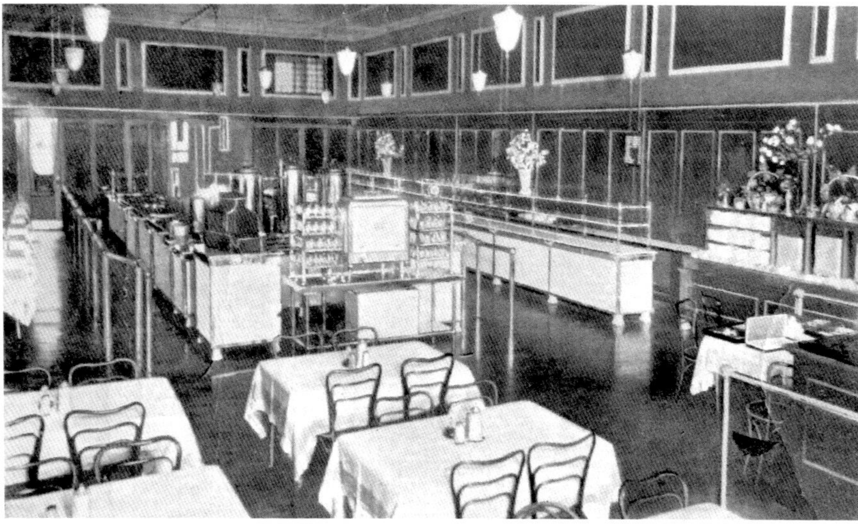

Postcard image of Britling Cafeteria featuring the famed steam table. *Courtesy of Steve Gilmer and What's on Second; photograph by Emily Brown.*

The feeling of excitement that must have permeated the city streets in the early 1900s would have been intoxicating, and it's no wonder the hard work required to run a restaurant couldn't dampen the spirit of industry in citizens of the young metropolis. Hard work and hospitality became two of the most prevalent virtues restaurateurs exhibited, and nowhere was that more evident than in the industrious Greek immigrants who found their way into the kitchens and dining rooms of Birmingham's new restaurants.

2

THE GREEK INFLUENCE

Like in the rest of America, a large immigrant population formed the backbone of the working class in Birmingham's early history. Large numbers of Greeks, in particular, found their way to Birmingham during the first part of the century. These immigrants were attracted by the promise of prosperous futures. The mining and steel boom created jobs and a chance to make a good living, prospects especially attractive to young men from Greece, which had recently been defeated in war by Turkey and whose market for crops like currants dried up across Europe and Russia, making work hard to come by. In contrast, mining, factory work and other pursuits, even in a land where they didn't speak the language, must have seemed like answers to prayers. These young men found their way across the Atlantic, mostly through family members already established in American businesses like grocery stores and restaurants large and small, and while many started out in big cities on the East Coast, significant numbers eventually found their way south and to Birmingham.

Over the years, Greeks in Birmingham found a particular affinity for restaurants and cooking, both fields that required long hours and hard work. Greek restaurateur Michael Matsos (of La Paree, Michael's Sirloin Room and Golden Rule BBQ), in a 2006 interview for the Southern Foodways Alliance, relayed how he noticed that almost all the Greeks he knew when he came to Birmingham in the 1940s were in the restaurant business. "They were dedicated, and they were willing to work," he said. "And that was the thing. And they stayed on top of it. And naturally, I had an edge on them because I was a university graduate and I understood the business sense. But still, it was very difficult to achieve some of the work the way they did. And they understood cooking because it was sort of handed down from their grandmothers and mothers and so forth, and they kept the recipes. Up to this day, some of the recipes are really hard to beat."

The Bright Star

One Greek family link to America and then Birmingham became known as the "Peleta Pipeline" because of the many men from the small village of Peleta who used family businesses, such as Peter T. Bonduris's Manhattan fruit stand, to help them gain their footing in their new country. In 1902, fourteen-year-old Tom D. Bonduris began working at his uncle's fruit stand, and after a brief return to Greece due to illness, he returned to America in 1906 and found his way to a job baking pies at a café called the Bright Star in Birmingham. Just a short year later, Bonduris took his savings and purchased his own restaurant in nearby Bessemer, borrowing the name the Bright Star Café. This restaurant, still in operation today, would be the one to bring the name to fame.

A small horseshoe-shaped bar, mosaic tile floor, barstools and a case of cigar boxes decorated the first Bright Star Café, which gained a reputation for serving good food at reasonable prices. The Peleta Pipeline brought Tom's brother Nick into the States in 1909, and as Nick joined his brother in business, the two prepared to move the Bright Star to its second and larger location. By 1911, the Bright Star Restaurant had moved to its third location, and in 1915, it had moved into its fourth and final location on the corner of Nineteenth Street and Third Avenue in Bessemer. Along the way, an uncle, Alexander, and another cousin, Gus Sarris, joined in the ownership as well. This location has become known for its mosaic tile floors, restored in the early 2000s; private booths that were built as the restaurant expanded into other parts of the building; and scenic murals, painted by a traveling German, that are mounted to the walls for diners to enjoy while eating.

Though not technically in Birmingham, the Bright Star deserves its place in local restaurant history not just because of its longevity but also because it exemplifies the work ethic, emphasis on family and hospitality and dedication to serving quality food that are so indicative of Birmingham restaurants that last. The early Bright Star was known for its coffee and doughnuts, cooked fresh each morning by Gus Sarris. In the 1920s, Bill Koikos came to America from Peleta and began working with his brother Pete, already established at the Bright Star. He reports that in those days, they served a thirty-five-cent vegetable plate, big bowls of soup, a seventy-five-cent steak, beef stew, oysters and catfish. When Tom Bonduris returned to Greece in the mid-1920s, the Koikos brothers became second-generation owners of the Bright Star, and Bill's sons, Jimmy and Nicky, carried on as owners, a role they still currently fill.

Hard times came to Birmingham and the surrounding areas during the Great Depression of the 1930s, and as demand for iron and steel dried up and jobs became scarce, dining out became harder and harder to afford. Bill Koikos has said that during the Depression when banks were closing, the Bright Star sometimes took in less than twenty dollars in a day and had trouble paying the rent. But through dedication, a little luck and coming to whatever agreements it could make on payment with vendors, the Bright Star stayed open through the hard times. Remarkably, it even found ways to be generous and lighten the load of customers whose loyalty it valued, even when those customers couldn't always afford a meal out. In those days, the back booths were draped with curtains so diners could enjoy meals in privacy, and when people came in asking for help or spare food, the Koikos and Bonduris families would take people into those back booths and feed

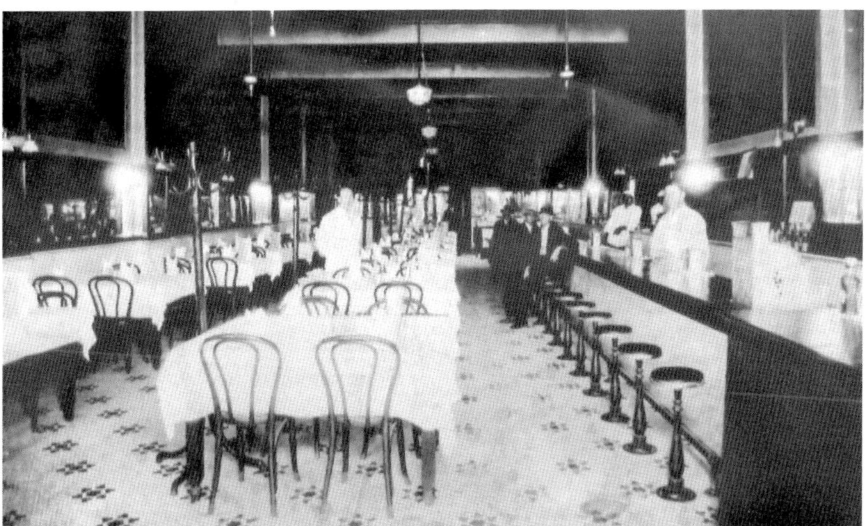

Fourth location of the Bright Star around 1915. Note the mosaic tile floor. *Courtesy of Bright Star Restaurant.*

them for free—whatever could be spared from the steam table, soup and even those famous donuts.

The Bright Star saw success during the 1940s and '50s, and in 1960, Jimmy Koikos got the call from his father that it was time to join the family business. Jimmy had been helping at the restaurant since the age of thirteen, sweeping floors and bussing tables, so he knew the business well. His younger brother, Nicky, joined in the partnership in 1968, and you can still find one or the other, or both, at the restaurant every day. Jimmy said he thinks the best thing to happen to the Bright Star during his and his brother's management is their expansion. They bought the building they'd been occupying since 1915 and have renovated and restored the restaurant, updating the kitchen and accounting system, modernizing with the times while staying true to the traditions of the restaurant. Before it became the popular choice, the Bright Star always focused on using the best, freshest ingredients. Its seafood, particularly the broiled Greek snapper or fried snapper throats they are now known for, is always fresh, never frozen. Jimmy relates with amusement the time a salesman tried to convince him to use portion-cut, flash-frozen snapper. He told the man he'd be wasting both their time. Fresh vegetables, not canned, accompany seafood specialties and the beloved Greek-style steak that won the Alabama Cattleman's Association Best Steak award in 2012. The Bright Star also has the distinction of being the only restaurant in Alabama to be honored as one of "America's Classics" by the James Beard Award Foundation.

These days their niece Stacey Craig and a nephew who grew up in Canada are poised to take the helm should Jimmy and Nicky ever step down, but Jimmy claims coming to work each day is like a vacation for him. He loves the work and the relationships he's built with his customers over the years. The emphasis Jimmy places on hospitality—greeting every customer, remembering regulars' anniversaries—is a huge part of the charm of the Bright Star, as is the history of the restaurant. Customers come in year after year, sitting at their favorite table with their favorite waitress, stopping by to chat with Jimmy or Nicky on their way out, and the rituals have become part of their own families' histories. Jimmy said he feels blessed to be at the Bright Star; he knows they've always worked hard, but they've also had a little luck. And both have contributed to their continued success.

John's Restaurant

Another restaurant famous for its Greek lineage is John's Restaurant on Twenty-first Street and First Avenue North. In the early 1900s, a young immigrant named John Proferis from near Sparta in Greece found his way to Birmingham on hearing that the South was the place to be and opened a restaurant called the Casino. The Casino gained a fast following, but the start of World War I forced John to change careers for a while. He turned to managing a dynamite plant. The restaurant bug never left him entirely, and in the early 1940s, John opened his fine-dining namesake restaurant, John's Restaurant, to immediate success. His daughter, Zoe, remembers patrons lining up for lunch from the very beginning and credits the success of the Casino to diners clamoring for more of John's food.

Aside from white tablecloths covering the Formica tables at night and wine and liquor available for those in celebratory moods, John's Restaurant distinguished itself with the still-at-the-time-novel option of fresh fish on the menu. A copy of an early menu to John's proclaims, "Our seafoods are received daily" as proudly as it does the fact that the restaurant had air conditioning. It's a sign of the times that John's was never considered a Greek restaurant, as ethnic food and culture had yet to be seen as desirous or of interest, yet various entrées, such as the Welsh Rabbit and Spanish Omelette, and cold plates like the "Imported Norwegian Sardines with Salad" did offer a bit of worldly flair. But a few Greek-style specialties found their way onto John's menu, and the uniqueness of their flavors ensured their popularity among Birmingham's steak-and-potatoes crowd. A Greek salad remained the only official nod to actual Greek cuisine, though the olive oil, lemon and oregano dressing the fresh fish certainly qualify for the Mediterranean diet. John invented a fish dish he called Trout Almondine that was a favorite, as were the cornbread and sweet rolls. Homemade shrimp gumbo also drew praises, as did the famous homemade French-style dressing topping John's slaw. When new owners took over John's Restaurant in the 1970s, John Proferis sold the rights to that famous dressing, which is still bottled and sold in stores today, though Zoe claims that version isn't the same as the original her father taught her how to make. Either way, most Birmingham residents know when you say "John's slaw," you're talking about finely shredded "angel hair" cabbage topped with thick, tangy orange dressing.

Zoe Cassimus, who is now a restaurateur in her own right with the Zoe's Kitchen franchises she started, fondly remembers how special going to her daddy's restaurant was as a young girl in the 1950s. She and her mother

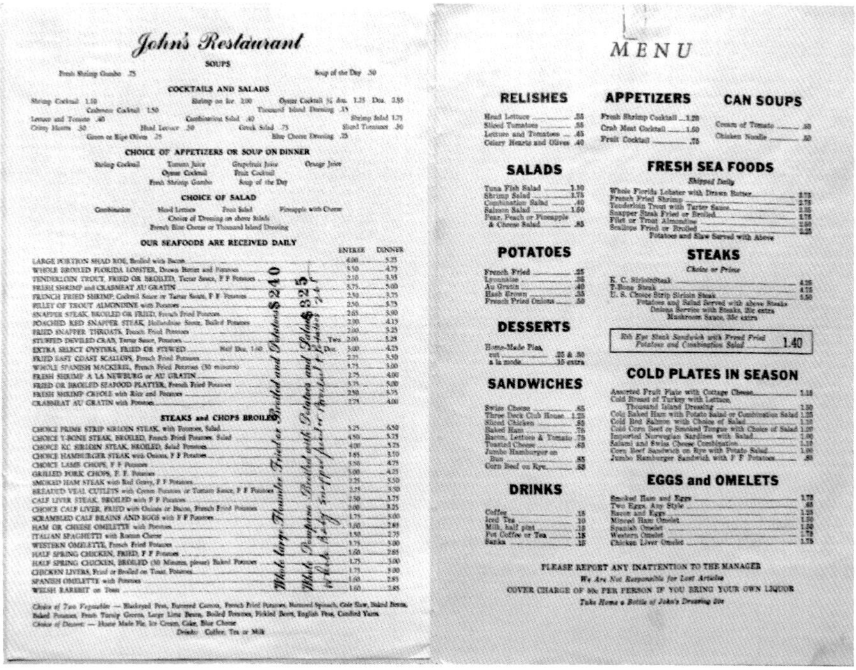

John's Restaurant

SOUPS

COCKTAILS AND SALADS

CHOICE OF APPETIZERS OR SOUP ON DINNER

CHOICE OF SALAD

OUR SEAFOODS ARE RECEIVED DAILY

STEAKS and CHOPS BROILED

MENU

RELISHES

APPETIZERS

CAN SOUPS

SALADS

FRESH SEA FOODS

POTATOES

STEAKS

DESSERTS

SANDWICHES

COLD PLATES IN SEASON

DRINKS

EGGS and OMELETS

John's Restaurant menu. *Courtesy of the Birmingham History Center; photograph by Emily Brown.*

would ride the bus downtown, catch a movie at the gorgeous and historic Alabama Theater and then come to the restaurant for dinner. Outside the restaurant, the vertical neon sign spelling out "John's" would have lit up the night sky. Her father ran the front of the house, so he could often be found checking on customers, making sure they were satisfied with their food, talking to the regulars and just being a good host in general. My own mother celebrated special occasions with her mother and father at John's Restaurant in the 1960s and '70s, as did many of her friends and neighbors in the suburbs of Birmingham.

Today, the newest owners of John's have revamped the menu and interior to reflect the changing demands of the modern customer. They've updated the name to John's City Diner, but they continue to serve a robust crowd for business lunches and dinners each week. In a nod to its history, you can still find a Greek salad, slaw and Trout Almondine at John's, but today, it might be served alongside organic, free-range chicken or pork, macaroni and cheese with exotic cheeses or even crispy duck.

Jeb's Seafood

In the 1930s and '40s, a particularly colorful man, one Augustus J. Jebeles—or "Mr. Jeb" to his customers—ran a successful seafood restaurant called Jeb's Seafood House that was host to the sports crowd. Also from Sparta, Greece, Jeb immigrated to America, at twelve years old, spending time in Nashville and El Paso, where he learned the restaurant trade, and Mexico, where he reportedly befriended Pancho Villa and dabbled in the film industry, before settling in Birmingham in 1918. Jeb founded the Dixie Coffee Company, which resided on Morris Avenue, before selling the business in 1925 to open the Reliance Hotel across from the Terminal Station. At the Reliance Hotel and Café, Jeb became known for great food that railroad men and newspaper reporters considered to be higher quality than some of the nicer restaurants downtown. After modernizing the space in the early 1930s, Jeb renamed the café Jeb's Seafood House, and it became a haunt of the sports crowd, who followed him when he moved to the First Avenue location that lasted until the early 1940s. Perhaps what Jeb is best known for, however, is his love of baseball. Jeb had always dreamed of owning a ball club, so when the chance came in 1943 to purchase the Birmingham Barons, he cashed in and did so. One of the owners of the Bright Star, John D. Bonduris, even sold his ownership there to join in at Jeb's Seafood House once Jeb sold the restaurant. Mr. Jebeles owned the Barons when they played at Rickwood Field and worked to establish their success until he sold the club in 1952, at the age of sixty-six. After years playing at a stadium in the suburbs, today's Birmingham Barons are back downtown at the new Regions Field, next to Railroad Park and across from Good People Brewing Company. In this location, the ball club is playing a significant role in bringing life, new business and even new restaurants back to the area.

The Fish Market

You can't talk about Greek families in Birmingham restaurants without mentioning the Fish Market and George Sarris. A seafood institution that's been around since the 1980s, and before when it was just a market for fish, the Fish Market downtown has always been known as the place to get fresh seafood at a reasonable price, whether that means fried crab claws or blackened Cajun-style catch of the day. With its roots as a literal market for fresh whole fish, the Fish Market still can be visited today, and customers can still pick up fish or shrimp to cook at home or sit down and enjoy a lunch or dinner of fresh seafood and sides.

As a young man, George Sarris found his way to Birmingham from his native Tsitalia in Greece, much like many of his neighbors and family. He began his restaurant career in Birmingham working in the kitchens of other Greek immigrants, places like Niki's, Niki's West and John's Restaurant. But in 1983, George decided to join his uncle at his wholesale fish market, Alabama Seafood, and open what was at first just a sandwich counter as part of the business. They changed the name to the Fish Market Restaurant, and George's career began in earnest. From the small market and restaurant on Twenty-first Street South to the large, airy building filled with wooden beams, nautical decorations and long, bright fish cases packed with ice that the restaurant now inhabits across the parking lot, the Fish Market has always been one of the best spots in Birmingham to enjoy fresh seafood at a fair price.

Back in Greece, George came from a culture that knew nothing of the farm-to-table movement and saw local produce as just produce—fresh and local were a way of life. George reminisces about the artichokes that grew six feet from his mother's kitchen window, the fig and apple trees that provided fresh fruit, foraging for mulberries in the mountains surrounding his home and the goats and sheep the family kept for milk, cheese and meat. Until he came to America in 1969, George had never tasted or even seen a canned green bean. Raised on cooking with the freshest ingredients and simple techniques and seasonings, George found a welcome home in Greek restaurant kitchens that were utilizing these techniques to prepare seafood sent in fresh from the Gulf. After all, he'd grown up attending a high school that was within walking distance of the ocean, from which his family harvested fresh seafood that he said was always easy to cook. Working at John's Restaurant, which helped put Birmingham on the map as a town for good seafood, George honed his skills and ideas about cooking fish the way he eventually would in his own restaurant, though there was always room for fried anything on the southern plate. It would be a while before the palate of Birmingham residents caught on in full to the health benefits of food prepared as it was back in Greece. But George maintains that the quality of ingredients makes the difference, no matter the preparation. "As long as it's fresh," he said. "Anything fresh is good, no matter if it's shark or snapper."

Access to those fresh ingredients, particularly quality seafood, became George's main goal at the Fish Market, so his first action as new owner was to purchase his own trucks to deliver seafood straight to his door. He also set about exposing Birmingham diners to new types of fish. Amberjack, in particular, was first served in the city from George's kitchen, as was tilapia, through a special arrangement with Auburn University's fish farming program. Now George estimates that with all the restaurant kitchens in Birmingham that serve tilapia, the city probably sees around 100,000 pounds each week. The other main change George has helped effect in Birmingham dining is the choice of healthy preparations for seafood dishes. He said when he started in the 1970s and '80s, about 90 percent of the customers wanted fried fish, shrimp, crab claws and oysters. Now the customers are almost 70 percent more likely to choose the healthier option of broiled or grilled.

The Fish Market menu currently offers fresh catches prepared on the grill, baked or served in its signature "Athenian" style with grilled onions, Greek olives, fresh tomatoes and feta cheese. You can find anything from a grilled amberjack po'boy and a classic Greek salad with grilled shrimp or fish to sushi-grade tuna steaks and the Fish Market's take on shrimp and grits. George credits Chef Frank Stitt of Highlands Bar and Grill with helping show customers how to eat fresher ingredients, making them demand better food across the city, and said that his own version of shrimp and grits is second best in the city, bested only by the dish on Highlands' menu.

Growing and adapting to the times and customers' changing palates is a large part of what has kept George successful in business for over thirty years. He believes restaurants that don't change die. George Sarris has been part owner in and responsible for helping start several other successful restaurants around town, and this philosophy translates to those businesses as well, keeping the Birmingham restaurant community healthy, flexible and strong. For instance, as part owner in the high-end Greek restaurant DoDiYos in the suburb of Homewood, George has been instrumental in helping to revamp the restaurant's menu and get it back to the basics of Greek cooking. Under George's instruction, DoDiYos is refocused on fresh ingredients, sometimes using eclectic ingredients like the goat of George's youth, taking in foraged produce and maybe even accepting vegetables from home farmers in trade for meals. Bartering backyard tomatoes for braised goat may be the wave of the future, but it's definitely a nod to how things were done in the simpler times of the past.

George Sarris's focus on quality has led him to source, bottle and import his own olive oil, which is used in the restaurant and available for purchase in the attached market. He's brought in olives from friends and family who have trees in Greece, and the trees he gets his figs from came over with his own father. Even George's brother brings in okra and heirloom tomatoes from his garden for the restaurant. A large part of sourcing local ingredients is knowing your farmer or producer, building relationships based on trust, which becomes easier when family completes that equation. George's son Dino works with him at the Fish Market today, learning the business from his father as George learned it from his family and continuing the traditions Birmingham restaurants have always been known for.

In addition to family always being a part of the Fish Market, George has sustained the practice of embracing the immigrant community in his kitchen and front of house. George shares that the staff of the Fish Market spans nine nationalities and speaks seven languages. Due to the draw of the University of Alabama at Birmingham and the attached medical school and hospital, students come to Birmingham, gain work visas and find a home in this community that is far more diverse than it was in the city's early years. At the Fish Market, George celebrates this diversity, relishing when his employees bring in spices, ingredients or flavors from home, all vehicles for the ever-moving wheel of change he loves. George still works long hours at the Fish Market and spends a good amount of time at DoDiYos as well, looking for that next shift he'll have to make to stay successful.

Hot Dogs

Perhaps due to the need for a quick and inexpensive lunch, early miners, factory workers and businessmen in Birmingham often found their way into one of the many hot dog stands cropping up in the city's buildings. These hot dog businesses were most often run by Greek immigrants who added their signature flavors to seasoned beef, chili and the special sauce that topped the griddle-cooked dogs settled into warmed or steamed buns. In addition to being a cheap meal, hot dog lunches or dinners had the advantage of being quick. A man could stand on the street and finish his dogs in just a few minutes before having to return to work. Proprietors could put the meals together fast as well, taking patron's orders for toppings—onions, mustard, sauerkraut and the sauce—with meat or chili and then wrap and bag the hot dogs with a bottled drink and chips before the next customer could make up his mind. Regulars might even find their order waiting when they entered the door if the owner had spied them coming from across the street. Everyone had their favorite hot dog stand, vouching that their preferred sauce was the best in the city, and this passion, coupled with the prevalence of hot dog businesses in various spots, made Birmingham synonymous with good food in hot dog form.

One of the first, if not the first, hot dog stands in Birmingham opened up on Second Avenue North and Nineteenth Street in 1919, named Tom's Coney's for its owner, Tom Kandilas. Young Tom found his way to Birmingham from a heavily Greek-populated area of Turkey known as Dardaelles. Upon entering the country in 1907, Tom operated a fruit stand in New York before making his way down to Plant City, Florida, to open a fruit and vegetable business. His young fiancée, Stella, waited back at home for Tom to establish himself, and as soon as he could, he returned to Dardaelles to wed and bring his bride to America. Poor Stella had a rough voyage, feeling more than common seasickness during her journey. But she was surprised to discover, upon quarantine at Ellis Island, that she was pregnant. When Tom and Stella's daughter, Katina, was three, they made their way to Birmingham and settled into the Greek church and community as best they could. As Katina entered school, Tom opened his hot dog stand, which would remain a family-run business for over fifty years.

Tom's Coney's was small, around seven feet wide by fifteen feet deep. Tom would stand behind the grill, serving up hot dogs to customers day and night. The famous seasoned beef, or "hot beef," that Birmingham dogs are known for, actually originated with Tom. In his elder years, Tom didn't have any teeth, and the hot dogs became too difficult to chew. He started cooking up some ground beef, seasoned with spices, onions and peppers, and put it on a hamburger bun for his dinner instead. The family suggested he top his hot dogs with this hot beef and call it a "special." He obliged, and a Birmingham tradition was born.

Tom's granddaughter Tasia remembers helping out in the restaurant during World War II. The French soldiers would file in, order their meals and eat out on the street because there wasn't enough room in the store for all of them. In those days, downtown Birmingham had a policeman stationed at every corner. Downtown was lively, full of shops and restaurants, movie theaters and general nightlife. The policemen kept things orderly and made friends with the business owners near their posts. Tasia tells a story of how many of the city's police force would come in for a meal around three thirty in the afternoon, and when she was helping, she thought she was supposed to give them all free hot dogs. Her grandfather quickly corrected her, letting her know that only their corner policeman got a free meal, but she said he was generally the type of generous man to give you his own shirt if you complimented it. Tasia also remembers her grandfather keeping a half pint of liquor beside the cash register on the counter, and favorite customers might have a nip poured into their Coke bottles if he was feeling festive. She relates that even during World War II, when the food supply was rationed, Tom's Coney's always had plenty of hot dogs, supplied by the local business Ziegler's that opened in the 1920s; plenty of buns and bread, from the local bread company Home Baking Co. (which currently sells buns and bread to local fast-food chains like Jack's and Milo's); and "Coca-Cola boxes stacked to the ceiling." The Coke relationship was a particularly good one, as Tasia claims responsibility for setting up their deliveryman with her friend who worked in the jewelry store across the street, leading to their eventual marriage.

During the Korean War, one of the young servicemen who often lined the block waiting for a chance to order one of Tom's Coney's dogs, a young Greek and military cook named Harry Pasisis on leave from Fort Rucker, met Tasia and fell in love. In 1953, before their impending marriage, Tom handed the keys to Tom's Coney's over to Harry, and the second generation of hard work and hot dogs began. Harry and Tasia's eldest son, Gus, said he helped out in the restaurant from the time he could walk. The restaurant was open seven days a week, from 7:00 a.m. to 10:00 or 11:00 p.m., serving the breakfast, lunch and dinner crowds as well as the after-theater crowds. When Gus was just twelve or thirteen years old, his parents left him in charge for the weekend when they went out of town on business. His grandmother would drop him off in the morning and pick him up around 7:00 p.m., and he handled it like a champ. During the civil rights era, Gus and Tom's Coney's saw many marches down Second Avenue, though the restaurant never had any protests or demonstrations in its own space, perhaps because the owners' ethnic minority made them less of a threat. Gus distinctly remembers during one march, policemen lined the street instead of just being stationed on the corners, and Martin Luther King Jr. walked right past their door.

Down the street, also on Second Avenue, another Greek-owned hot dog stand had begun in 1939, though the building had been in use as a different restaurant since before the First World War. Pete Koutroulakis opened Pete's Famous Hot Dogs in a space not much bigger than Tom's Coney's and hung outside the famous blue neon sign that now resides at Barber Motorsports Museum. The sign reportedly cost him $500, a small fortune at the time. After Pete took ill in 1948, Pete's nephew Constantine, known as Gus to all, took over operations and remained behind the counter for twelve to fifteen hours a day until his death in 2011. Gus Pasisis said there was always a lot of unspoken competition among the local hot dog businesses, but a lot of love and respect came with that competition as well. He tells a story of how his dad would send him down the street to Pete's to "borrow a cup of sugar" and instruct him to count the bread boxes in Pete's Famous to see how their business was doing. The next day, Gus Koutroulakis would be down at Tom's Coney's for his cup of sugar, counting their boxes just the same. But aside from mild-mannered business rivalries, the families were close and connected. Gus Koutroulakis's sisters were in the Pasisis wedding, and his brother was the godfather for one of the Pasisis children. The sauces and seasonings of the two restaurants were what made them different, and according to Gus Pasisis, customers who were loyal to one would swear the other tasted like garbage.

During the 1980s, the atmosphere downtown changed. Businesses and restaurants had moved out to the suburbs, and the Pasisis family finally decided to close. They kept the rights to their secret sauce and recipes, and to this day, Gus said his mother asks him weekly about doing something more with the business, either opening up another hot dog stand or bottling the sauce. It's no wonder she's held on to this love for the business; it encompassed her whole life. Gus is proud of what his parents and great-grandparents did. That hot dog stand put him and his two brothers through college. He said his father taught him that if you want anything in life, you pay for it yourself, a lesson he learned for himself when he worked at the restaurant as his first paying job out of college. Eventually, Gus decided he wanted to do something other than sell hot dogs for a living, and he found his way to his current marketing career in part through writing Tom's Coney's ads for the local radio station WZZK. Gus's dad, Harry, never lost his love for the restaurant business and the busy, hardworking lifestyle that comes with it. Though Harry Pasisis hasn't stood behind the grill at Tom's Coney's for a long time, he still keeps a hand in the restaurant game by helping out in the kitchen of Jim 'N Nick's, the barbecue restaurant started by another Greek family. Harry goes in for a few hours a few days a week to prep in the Jim 'N Nick's kitchen. And the Pasisis family still gets together to enjoy hot dogs at home, with Harry cooking up a batch of the special sauce and hot beef to go on top.

Other notable hot dog stands in Birmingham's past include the Lyric, which is also gone to make way for the renovation of the Lyric Theater; Gus's Hot Dogs, currently still open on Fourth Avenue and doing a brisk business; and the original Sneaky Pete's, which has many franchises and bottles and sells its sauce. Though so many of our beloved hot dog stands have closed, there's still hope for Birmingham's hot dog future. Joining the

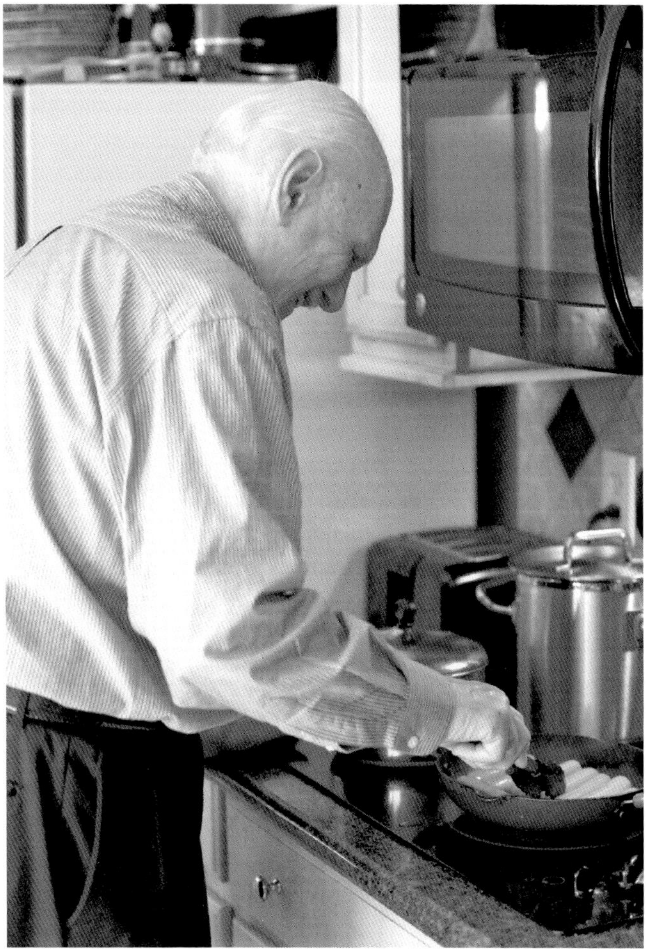

Harry Pasisis preps hot beef and hot dogs. *Photograph by Arik Sokol.*

food truck scene for a time in the appropriate form of a cart, Ferocious Dogs, run by Pete Szelenbaum and Josh Kelly, was a pop-up cart available for parties, events and local businesses to reserve. Employees of neighborhood favorite Rojo, Pete and Josh also held monthly hot dog nights at Rojo on Mondays, when the kitchen was closed. Ferocious Dogs served a classic hot dog, but it also offered fusion twists on toppings, including báhn mì, Reuben style and even veggie dogs. Though Ferocious Dogs held its last hot dog night in early 2015, its continuation and update of a Birmingham tradition was notable for carrying a little torch for the hot dog stands of old and gives hope for more hot dog innovation in the city's future.

3

SOUTHERN FARE

For most of the rest of the country, southern cooking has always been synonymous with soul food. Collards and ham hocks cooked slow and low, thick and creamy macaroni and cheese, candied yams as sweet as dessert, black-eyed peas simmered long enough that they're softer than butter, crispy-on-the-outside yet crumbly-on-the-inside cornbread and various beefy or porky bits roasted, smoked, simmered and fried have come to symbolize the long drawl of the South and hot days cooled by nothing better than an icy class of syrupy tea. And while it's true that the modern South has more to offer in terms of variety and style of cooking, there will always be a warm and welcome place for the sort of roots cooking that today's meat-and-three, steam table or soul food restaurants serve up on a daily basis around Birmingham. These restaurants, most often family owned and serving family recipes, have been feeding generations of Birmingham families since the 1950s.

Eagle's

One of these family-owned establishments, Eagle's Restaurant, is nestled in a small community just north of downtown near the large ACIPCO (American Cast Iron Pipe Company) factory and has been serving the neighborhood and the rest of the city delicious food since 1951. The small gray cinderblock

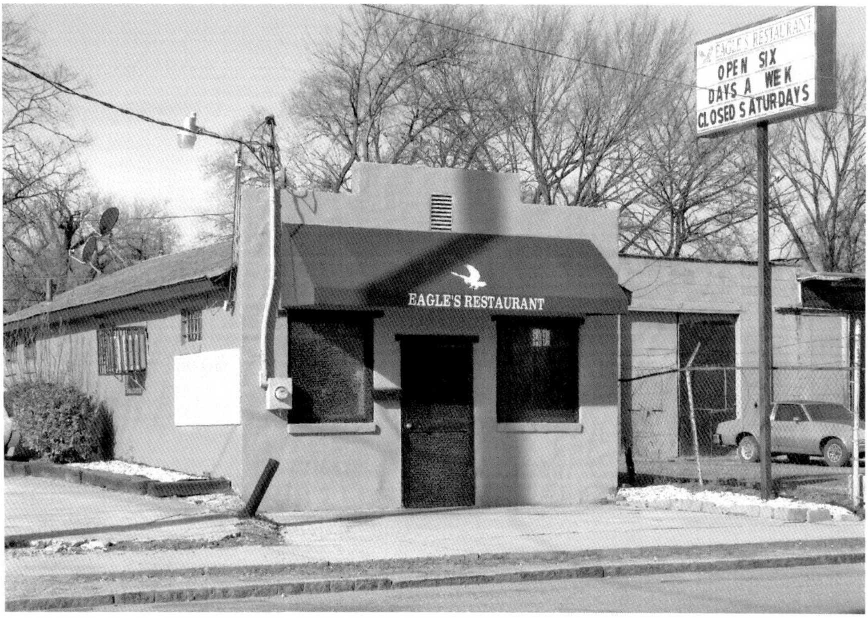

Outside Eagle's Restaurant in 2015. *Photograph by Emily Brown.*

building housing Eagle's is unassuming, and those unfamiliar to the area might have to keep a sharp eye out to avoid driving past. But the stop in, to sit at one of the few tables inside the small restaurant or grab a takeout lunch like many of the ACIPCO workers do, not only satisfies hunger but also creates a desire to keep coming back for more. Even Chef Chris Hastings of Hot and Hot Fish Club has said that Eagle's soul food is "amazing."

In the 1950s, the family who ran the restaurant served a brisk business of hamburgers and those ubiquitous Birmingham hot dogs. When the original family sold out to the family of the current owners, one condition was that the name remain the same. "That was one of the selling points," said Ahmad Rucker, whose father purchased the business in 1974 and who now runs the restaurant with his mother and his sisters. When Ahmad's mother, Delores Banks, took over from his father in 1993, she steered the restaurant toward serving exclusively soul food as it does today. Ahmad believes Eagle's biggest secret is the good will of its community. "When you come in here it's like you're a part of our family. No frills," he said. "I guess that's what brings people back, along with the food. It's soul food cooking scratch daily, using fresh vegetables from the farmers market [Finley Market] down the street. We have a strong supply chain. It just works."

Eagle's original cook, responsible for most of the recipes for food like oxtails, baked chicken and dressing, neck bones with potatoes and beef tips with rice, passed her culinary secrets down to Delores, who's the head cook today. Delores learned those recipes but definitely put her own spin on them—"to perfect them," said her son. Ahmad joined the restaurant's family team when he graduated from college in 2006 and notes that the menu, which rotates specials on a daily basis, has stayed pretty much the same the entire time. "It's like clockwork. It just works," he said. "We don't really change much."

Ahmad believes this stability and the family-friendly atmosphere are some of the restaurant's biggest assets. "It's a family-run restaurant from the front to the back," he said, and he jokes that regulars might even get a glimpse of "brother/sister rivalries going on" with him and his sister at the serving and cash register line. "We're real people, and we love serving the community. I know I'm going to be doing this for the rest of my life," Ahmad said. "We're committed to our craft, and I think it shows in our products. I hope people come out and try Eagle's." Hospitality and graciousness are a big part of Eagle's business, and Ahmad expresses thanks for the business his family has built together and the customers that have stayed with them over the years. "We try to make sure we say thank you. You're going to hear 'Thank you' two or three times when you're here," he said. "My sister, me, we appreciate the business. I just want to continue to put good quality food on the steam table and say thank you." Like so many of Birmingham's restaurants, established and new, quality eats are best served with graciousness like Ahmad and his family's.

The stability, longevity and quality of Eagle's has even gained it a bit of national attention. In 2013, Travel Channel celebrity Andrew Zimmern visited Eagle's to try its oxtails for an episode of his television show *Bizarre Foods America*. The visit and accompanying press have brought in business from people, including Birmingham locals previously unfamiliar with the area, who might not otherwise have heard of the restaurant in its quiet neighborhood.

Green Acres

One Birmingham institution has the distinction of being one of the first African American–owned businesses in the city and has made an indelible mark on its neighborhood not only with its own success but also through

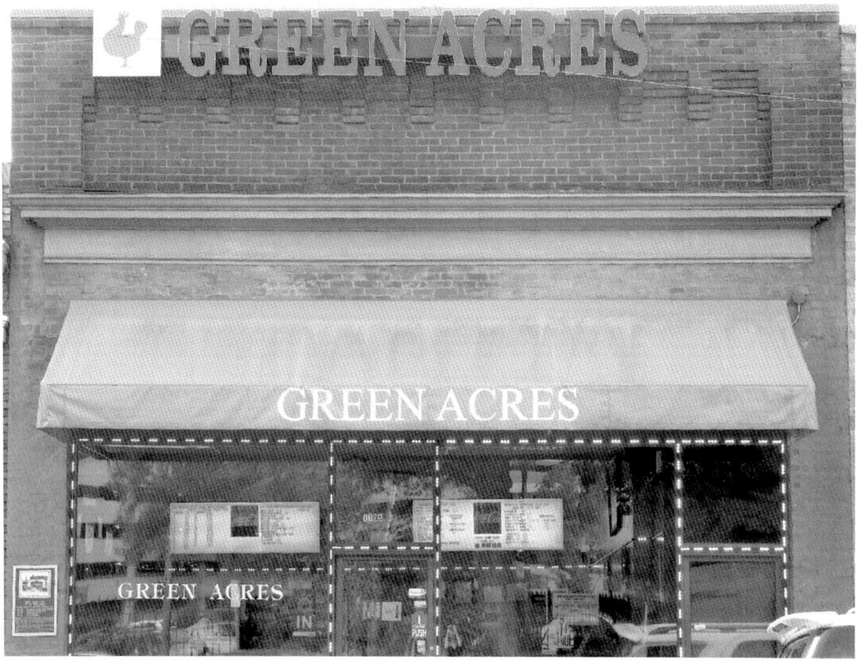

Outside Green Acres in 2015. *Photograph by Emily Brown.*

the efforts of its owners to support a thriving district. Green Acres Café on Fourth Avenue North opened in 1958 and has been serving its signature chicken wings to eager crowds ever since. People who have been coming to eat at Green Acres since they were children walk in the door almost every day, and now they're bringing their own kids in to continue the tradition.

Birmingham in 1958 wasn't anything close to being a friendly place for an African American, with strict segregation laws and rampant discrimination. If African Americans went looking to get a bite to eat at a restaurant, they couldn't eat in the dining room or even walk through the front door for service. They had to come to the back doors to order food and eat elsewhere. Charles Gratton, who had worked in delivery for the Coca-Cola bottling company and would have seen more than his fair share of this discrimination, decided to open a place where African Americans could come in and enjoy a meal. The youngest of ten children who grew up in a small house on the back side of the white Norwood neighborhood and had to walk six miles to elementary school each day instead of being allowed to go to the white school a block and a half over, Charles was no stranger to the unfair way things were handled in the South. Some of his other siblings moved north to Chicago and found success; one of them operated four prosperous restaurants there, all named Green Acres. Another brother opened up a Green Acres in North Birmingham in 1950, so when Charles decided to open his own business, the restaurant and the name were a natural fit.

Popular menu items at the time included quarter chickens, either white meat breast and wing or dark meat leg and thigh. But customers who preferred white meat tended not to want the wing portion, even asking Charles to cut that piece off before the chicken was served. Greg Gratton, who grew up in his father's restaurant and now runs it himself, remembers his father's frustration with the waste of all those chicken wings. Charles told his wife they needed to stop throwing away the wings and that he was going to come up with a solution to get people to want them. Thus, the two-wing basket was born—two whole wings, served with French fries and a piece of white bread, all for $0.35. Today, you can get the same special for just $2.35.

At this time, the restaurant was still in its original location, on Sixth Avenue North and Sixteenth Street, right across from the historic Sixteenth Street Baptist Church. The restaurant stayed there until the bombing blew out all its windows.

"That was devastating," Greg said. Weary and hungry protestors had been known to stop in for a meal after sit-ins and demonstrations, finding Green Acres to be a peaceful and welcoming haven. The family kept going after the bombing, however, and moved the restaurant to Fourth Avenue, across the street from its current location, where it had a lounge that served beer to patrons in the back. In a 1994 interview with Duke University, Charles Gratton recalled the struggles of the 1960s and the change Dr. Martin Luther King Jr. brought with his message and actions. Charles said hearing Dr. King speak made him "feel like [King] was touching the inside of me." Through Dr. King's and other protestors' efforts, true integration did eventually come to Birmingham and its restaurants, and during that upheaval, Green Acres remained open to serve.

In 1970, Green Acres moved once again, next door to the current location, and stayed there until 1991, when, through the efforts of Mayor Richard Arrington, Charles was given the opportunity to purchase his own building. Most of the real estate in this area of Fourth Avenue had been owned by absentee landlords, people who weren't investing in upkeep or repairs or the health of the neighborhood. The mayor started a land bank program in the 1980s to help African American business owners purchase their own buildings. Now, the entire block of businesses is owned and run by African Americans. The city even put up a plaque on the street commemorating Charles Gratton's contribution to the neighborhood and the civil rights movement.

Greg Gratton came to own his father's restaurant after living in California for many years, raising his family and working for the Southern California Gas Company. With his wife, he'd often come back to Birmingham to visit their families, and on one visit, Greg noticed how much his father's health had deteriorated. When he was growing up, the restaurant had been his home, and with his business background, Greg was in the perfect position to take over for his father. When he was younger, he and his siblings would walk or catch a bus after school and come down to the restaurant to work. They'd peel one-hundred-pound sacks of potatoes, cut them up for French frying and then put them to soak in five-gallon tubs of water to keep them from turning brown. With the potato preparation, the Gratton children would also get the wings ready for the restaurant's need to last until the next day. Then they'd sit down at the restaurant to do their homework before walking home. Greg said he knows that his father, who passed away in 1999, would be proud of the work he's doing in the restaurant today, work that includes carrying on his dream of franchising Green Acres.

At one point, Charles Gratton considered buying a franchise of several different brands of fast-food chains, but Greg convinced him that he'd been running his own successful business long enough that he ought to franchise Green Acres instead. Neither knew much about franchising, so Greg took himself to the Birmingham library to do some research, consulted with lawyers in Southside to draw up a franchising contract and trademarked their logo: a rooster and the slogan "Try it, you'll like it." In the late 1990s and early 2000s, Green Acres had ten franchised restaurants across the city. A few of those businesses didn't live up to the standards Greg had set, and he was forced to revoke their franchises; however, five still remain, three of them run by Greg, his wife and his family.

Aside from the legendary wing deals, Green Acres also serves breakfast sandwiches with egg and sausage or thick-cut bologna, which is grilled and served on toast or a hamburger bun with lettuce and tomato. The center-cut pork chop sandwich is also a hit, as are the whiting and catfish. Fried green tomatoes always receive praise, and they can be ordered as a side or as part of the Manager's Special, which also includes wings and fries, for eight dollars.

Along with his restaurant duties—from which he officially retired last year when he passed the reins to his daughter, though he's still around to help out when needed—Greg sits on the board of Urban Impact, a nonprofit dedicated to promoting economic growth in the Fourth Avenue District, something else that would have made his father proud. The group gives tours of the district, taking visitors to the Civil Rights Institute and showing them other important landmarks and buildings in the neighborhood. Greg said God has blessed him, and it's clear he's enjoying the success and growth of his business, his neighborhood and his family. "To be in business this long," Greg said, "you've got to be doing something right. You've got to be serving good food, and you've got to be treating people right."

Ted's Restaurant

The other side of Greek restaurants in Birmingham that still has a big impact on the culinary landscape today is one with especially southern roots: the meat-and-three or steam table restaurant. Institutions across the city have been serving up fried chicken, fried okra, fried green tomatoes, chopped steak, collard or turnip greens, candied yams, cornbread, macaroni and cheese and more for decades, providing southern comfort at fair prices in unassuming settings, all with a friendly smile.

One such establishment has been in business since 1973, run by just two Greek families and specializing in the usual steam-table fare plus Greek specialties like Greek-style chicken and potatoes, souvlaki and pastitsio. Ted's Restaurant on Twelfth Street South was named for the original owner, Ted Sarris, who ran the small restaurant for almost thirty years with his wife, Litsa. Like the Fish Market's George Sarris, who was actually a nephew of his, Ted came to America from Tsitalia. He'd learned his cooking skills working for years on passenger ships in the Mediterranean, and after making it to first cook, Ted arrived in the States, where his uncle Jim Sarris was already running a successful restaurant in Birmingham called Old Hickory Restaurant. Ted established himself in Birmingham at the Old Hickory, eventually purchasing the restaurant from his uncle before returning to Greece to find and marry his bride. Aside from bringing his love and business partner back from that fateful trip to Greece, Ted also decided to bring more of the flavors of his home country to America and even claims to be the first man in the city to do so. Southerners took their time adjusting to these new tastes, but Ted's persistence paid off eventually. These Greek menu items have become favorite staples just as much as the meatloaf.

Old Hickory Restaurant's lease ended in 1972, but Ted and Litsa had already purchased the property where the current restaurant still stands, and

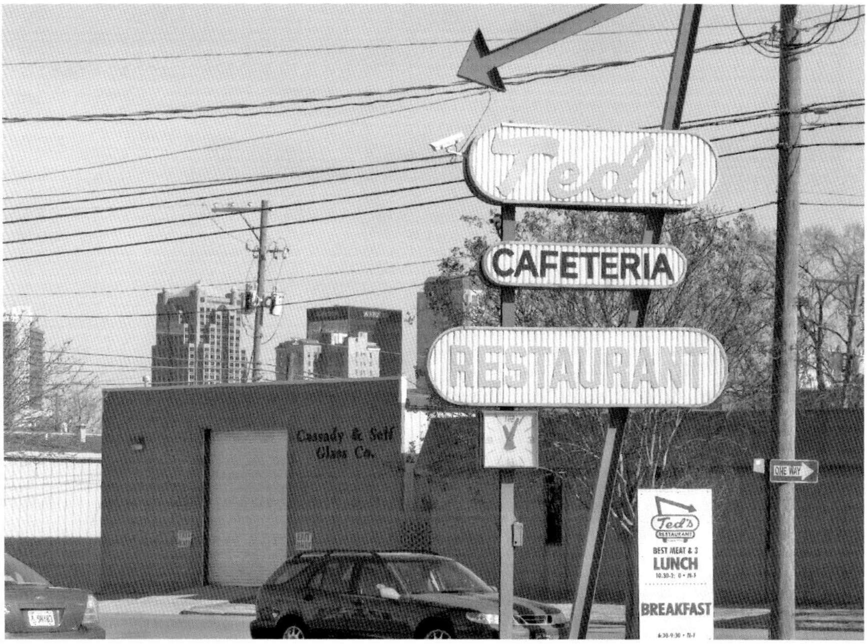

Sign pointing to Ted's Cafeteria Restaurant in 2015. *Photograph by Emily Brown.*

they lost no time building the new Ted's Old Hickory Restaurant. Always a man who valued religion and family above all else, Ted never opened on Sundays, but the family did work together six days a week from 6:00 a.m. to 10:00 p.m. until the birth of their two children. At that time, they decided opening five days a week for breakfast and lunch would better fit their lifestyles.

At the age of seventy, Ted started to think about retiring, which was when, while planning his birthday celebration at the Hoover Country Club, he met Tasos Toupoulis. Like himself, Tasos had immigrated to America from Greece, but Tasos had earned a degree in aerospace engineering from the University of Alabama before finding his way to restaurant and country club kitchens. Ted sold the restaurant to Tasos, insisting that Tasos's wife, Beba, work at his side just as Litsa had worked with him. Tasos and Beba collaborated with Ted and Litsa during the transition. The Sarrises shared secret recipes and techniques, and the Toupoulises met loyal customers, ensuring the quality and traditions regulars had come to expect would remain the same. Aside from putting their own spin on a few recipes and shortening the name to just Ted's Restaurant, Tasos and Beba have maintained everything, even the cash register. With three young children of their own, the Toupoulis family has continued to embody the values that helped establish Ted's Restaurant as the go-to spot for the diverse downtown crowd of bankers, construction workers, lawyers, doctors, nurses and policemen on the hunt for good food and warm service.

Niki's/Niki's West

Since their openings in the 1950s—long before the "buy local" movement took the country by storm—two other Greek-owned meat-and-three restaurants, Niki's and Niki's West, have been supporting local farmers by buying their produce. Originally opened by John and Margaret Hontzas in 1951 and 1957 and named for their youngest daughter, Niki, the downtown location is now owned by George Sissa, who purchased the restaurant from the Hontzas family in the 1980s, and Niki's West is owned by John's great-nephews Pete and Teddy Hontzas.

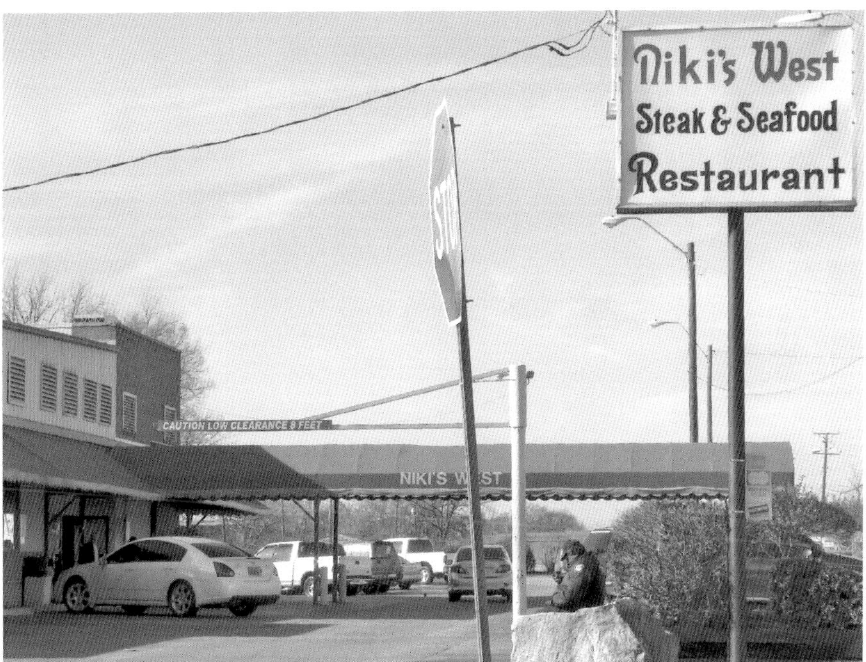

Outside Niki's West in 2015. *Photograph by Emily Brown.*

John Hontzas arrived in the United States in the 1900s, settling in Jackson, Mississippi, and opening a restaurant known as Johnny's Place that served meat-and-three-style food. In 1950, John and his wife decided to expand and open another restaurant in Birmingham, perhaps because of the strength of the Greek culture in the city, and chose a spot downtown on Second Avenue because, at that time, it was right across from the farmers' market. The idea for Niki's was to support the rural farmers who drove their pickups in each day to sell their fresh eggs, greens, potatoes and more. The Hontzas family would buy the produce and then turn around and serve it at the restaurant, which was a small spot offering a handful of meat dishes accompanied by a dozen vegetable choices. But when the farmers' market moved to its current location on Finley Avenue in the mid-1950s, John and Margaret were concerned they'd lose their connection with the growers. The second location on Finley seemed to be the perfect solution to maintain this early version of farm-to-table dining. As business grew, with both locations serving blue- and white-collar workers, keeping up with restaurants in two different states became too difficult for John and Margaret, so they brought in nephews to run each restaurant.

Niki's Downtown was given to George Hontzas and his brothers, who are also credited with helping start John's Restaurant and Alabama Seafood, which eventually became the Fish Market Restaurant. After his brothers' passing in the 1980s, George Hontzas sold the restaurant to George Sissa. George Sissa's father taught him the restaurant business from a young age, so he was a natural fit to take over the successful family-run venture. The senior Sissa, Nicholas, had arrived in the United States from Greece at the age of seventeen, soon serving in World War I. Nicholas traveled extensively across America, but in Birmingham, he fell in with a group of fellow Greeks who impressed him with their hospitality and friendship. In an interview with Amy Evans in 2004 for the Southern Foodways Alliance, George relates a story his father told him that might be the key to explaining the prevalence of Greek immigrants in the restaurant business in Birmingham:

> *When they came from Greece, nobody would hire them. So they took…the jobs nobody else wanted. And they couldn't afford to live anywhere, so there'd be four or five guys together, and they'd rent one room. And they would alternate the cooking chores. Like on a Monday it would be…Nick Sissa, or Tuesday it would be Sarris, Wednesday it might have been Hontzas…And he told me that's how they developed a competitiveness between each other to see who could come up with a better dish every night. And from there, some of them*

> *started opening up little fruit stands. And then they started little snack bars with sandwiches.*

Nicholas owned several restaurants across the city, including a place called Nick's Café across from the current University of Alabama–Birmingham (UAB) Hospital and a place called Terminal Café across from the Terminal Station.

George Sissa grew up in these restaurants and said that the business was in his blood. So when the opportunity came to purchase Niki's, already a Birmingham favorite, he took it. George Sissa expanded the menu at Niki's, which now serves thirteen meat choices daily, from the usual southern fare to Greek specialties like pastitsio, Greek chicken and souvlaki. Vegetable options number in the thirties each day and are cooked in the Greek, rather than southern, style, with no meat. Everything—even the eight different varieties of pies—is made from scratch daily, and George said the consistency and quality of the food is what keeps customers coming back, year after year. He enjoys checking in on the customers while they dine, asking about the food, and their responses are generally that the food is great, exactly what they have come to expect.

Across town at Niki's West, after deciding to pass the restaurant responsibility along to another family member, John and Margaret sent for their nephew Gus Hontzas to take over. In the old days, Niki's West was small, more of a truck stop or roadside café than the large restaurant it evolved into over the years. Farmers might stop in for breakfast before selling their produce at the market across the street or for a bite of lunch before heading home. At one point the restaurant stayed open twenty-four hours a day and reportedly kept its doors open during a snowstorm so truckers seeking shelter could have something warm to eat. Known for its fresh vegetables, like the Niki's downtown, the new restaurant soon gained a following from surrounding neighborhoods north, east and west of Birmingham, where a lot of residential areas had grown. The viability of the area even led Gus's brother, Theo, to open up another meat-and-three restaurant down the street, the Smokehouse, which is also still in operation. To set Niki's West apart and draw in the crowds looking for evening entertainment in the 1960s, Gus eventually added in the back a large lounge area, where they served alcohol and offered entertainment in the form of go-go dancers—not quite the family-friendly atmosphere they're known for today.

Through his cousin who ran the downtown Niki's, Gus met his wife, Betty, a woman of Greek heritage who had also grown up in the restaurant business.

Her father's small café on Second Avenue was called the Three Star Café. In her Southern Foodways Alliance interview, Betty joked that growing up around restaurants, seeing the hard work and personal sacrifice it took to make a dollar, made her swear she'd never marry a restaurant man, or a Greek, or someone with black hair, but she ended up with a man who was all three. Betty raised their children at home until the late 1970s, when Gus's partner left the restaurant and she offered to help out on the cash register for a few weeks until her husband could find a replacement. Gus must have liked having Betty there because he never found that replacement, and her few hours in the restaurant before picking the kids up from school turned into a full-time job eventually. In the 1980s, in an effort to find something that would draw the downtown crowds back out, Gus began a series of remodels and expansions to the restaurant. First, he built a large dining room, and then the lounge was eliminated to make way for an improved kitchen with dedicated areas for baking, salad preparation, storage and dishes. A second dining room was added in the back, and the front entrance was remodeled, which is what customers see when they visit the restaurant today.

Gus passed away in 2001, so now his sons, Pete and Teddy, run the day-to-day operations, serving breakfast, lunch and dinner from the steam table as well as their à la cart menu that's famous for seafood, usually broiled in the Greek style, with lemon and butter. Chef Chris Hastings of Hot and Hot Fish Club mentioned Niki's West as one of the cool places in Birmingham he's always loved to visit because it's consistently been a "good, simple place to go, with all the foods from the farmers market." And in addition to the vegetables, which still come from local farmers as much as possible, Niki's West has become known for its brand of Greek chicken, even though it serves a mean barbecue chicken as well. Niki's West even serves three different types of okra—fried, boiled with onions and bell peppers and Greek style, with tomatoes. Pete makes the point that a lot of people assume dishes prepared with tomatoes are Italian, but in fact, many traditional Greek dishes are also full of tomatoes. During his interview with Amy Evans for the Southern Foodways Alliance, Pete told Amy that he thinks there's a definite appeal to Niki's style of cooking, southern with Greek flair. He claims to be able to tell when first-time customers come from north of the Mason-Dixon line because they're not used to the type and number of vegetables that are plentiful in the South. Steering them away from more basic potatoes, carrots and peas, Pete suggests new customers try the fried okra and collard greens to start, promising they can send them back if they don't love them as much as he expects they will.

Birmingham's brand of southern food is unique in its inclusiveness. What defines southern cooking in Birmingham can include everything from greens cooked all day and served up with biscuits and fried pork chops to the Mediterranean flavors of a broiled snapper enjoyed with a mess of stewed okra and tomatoes and topped off with a slice of silky chocolate pie. No other city in the region can claim such rich Greek and American heritage, after all. Without these families sending their hard work out the kitchen door and onto a plate generation after generation, we might have lost our roots to the food that does truly feed the soul. Eating in these restaurants, tasting the same flavors our grandparents enjoyed, keeps a part of the past alive. None of these restaurants is especially fancy, and that's not what keeps customers coming back. It's tasting that tradition, walking in and ordering the same squash dish our parents ordered for us as children and knowing it will be the same, just as fresh, just as good. It's seeing the same faces, maybe a little older but with the same smile and the same friendly service. It's food cooked honestly and simply that keeps us returning.

4

THE ORIGINS OF FINE DINING

Though fine dining is far more traditional in definition than Birmingham's current restaurant scene full of seasonal and local ingredient–focused high-end restaurants, the city does have some history of fine dining beyond slightly stuffy French food served in grand hotels. In a time before the American palate craved salsa as its condiment of choice and before the health benefits of olive oil and raw foods became all the rage, white tablecloth restaurants were most likely to serve steak-and-potatoes fare to their eager patrons. Of course, being Birmingham, seafood continued to occupy a large portion of the menus as well. But diners were also expanding their horizons to meals outside their own cultural backgrounds, relishing everything from new and romantic Italian specialties to exotic cuisine from China. Early fine dining in the Magic City laid the groundwork for a city that has become known for adventurous diners who crave quality.

Michael Matsos

After World War II, Birmingham's downtown dining scene became a place known not only for good, fresh seafood and quality steaks but also restaurants that specialized in an upscale atmosphere where average diners might even mingle with local and national celebrities. One such restaurant, conveniently located down the block from the Tutwiler Hotel

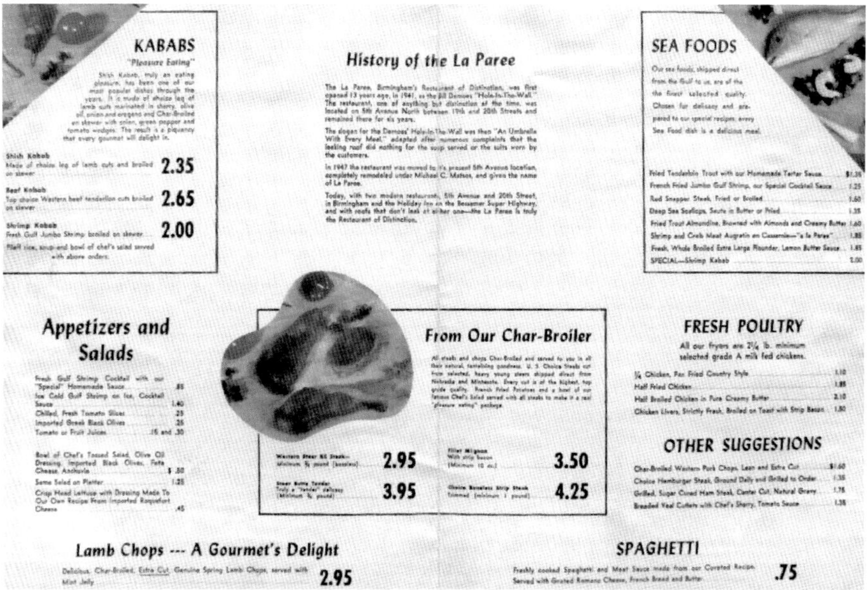

La Paree menu. *Courtesy of the Birmingham History Center; photograph by Emily Brown.*

on Fifth Avenue North, came about from the partnership of a second-generation Greek immigrant, Michael Matsos, and his partner and chef, Bill Demoes, yet another Greek with good cooking in his blood. The two opened La Paree in the 1940s, and it quickly became known among politicians as the place to get a well-cooked steak or new delicacies like shish kabob, pilaf rice and spaghetti with burnt butter. La Paree has even been credited with bringing the first dish of baked lamb onto a Birmingham table. Michael used to follow Bill Demoes around the kitchen, watching him work and writing down recipes, ready to step in should he ever have to take time off. And while Bill worked the kitchens, he began sponsoring family members back in Greece to come to America, where he put them to work in the restaurant.

Born in 1918 in Massachusetts and raised in New York, Matsos was a businessman first and foremost. He'd chosen the University of Alabama's Commerce School for college because research led him to believe it was the best buy for his money. During the war, he'd worked as an air traffic controller, but he longed to get back to his business roots. So when the opportunity arose to open La Paree, he was ready. One tale of his business acumen involves the doorman from the Tutwiler, whose job it was, in part, to help park guests' cars. Michael struck a deal with the doorman, named

Albert, that if he'd steer hotel guests to La Paree for their night on the town, he could eat at the restaurant for free anytime he wanted.

Eventually, Michael felt Bill needed the restaurant to support his expanded family, so he sold him his share in 1953 and went out on his own to open Michael's Sirloin Room in the nearby community of Bessemer through his association with the new hotel chain Holiday Inn. Holiday Inn opened its fifth hotel on the Bessemer Super Highway, with Michael's Sirloin Room attached, a prime location that helped the restaurant gain popularity for the same recipes he'd served at La Paree. Michael continued to work with hotel chains, opening Michael's Sirloin Rooms in Huntsville and Madison in northern Alabama throughout the 1950s. In 1958, Michael opened a location in Birmingham's Southside community, across from the Parliament House, which became his flagship restaurant, known for his steer butt steak as much as the chance to rub elbows with sports celebrities like Alabama's Coach Paul "Bear" Bryant or Hollywood celebrities like Bob Hope. Crowds came in for dinner after football games at Legion Field, and the restaurant was a favorite of local sports reporter Henry "Zipp" Newman. In a 2006 interview, Matsos recalls how "all the different cultures and everything used to hang out at Michael's back in those days." One customer, Jabo Stone, the owner of a little barbecue joint called Golden Rule in nearby Irondale, used to visit Michael's frequently, which led to Matsos eventually purchasing his restaurant and franchising it across the Southeast. In the early 1990s, Matsos sold Michael's, but you can still get a steer butt steak at Michael's Steak and Seafood at the Aloft Hotel in downtown Homewood.

Eating in Style in the 1950s

Other than visiting one of Michael Matsos's establishments to celebrate a night in style, Birmingham residents could also choose from a few other fine-dining restaurants when they desired a nice meal. Neither Dales Cellar Restaurant, famous for its steaks, nor Cobb Lane Restaurant, known for French-style flair, exists any longer, but both are remembered fondly. The Club, Birmingham's beautiful private club perched atop Red Mountain, still hosts diners and events, perhaps a credit to its willingness to evolve with the times, changing just about everything but its delectable sticky orange rolls.

Dales Cellar, so named because the restaurant resided in the cellar of the apartment building it occupied, was opened in 1946 by Jacob "Jake" Levine

Jr. Dale's eventually expanded to nine locations across six regional cities, and its famous seasoning can still be purchased at grocery stores today. What set Dale's apart started as a joke from a loyal customer and friend of Jake's who asked to have his meal prepared "right here, right now, at the table!" Jake obliged, bringing a hibachi grill out tableside and cooking the man's steak in front of him. This stunt led to building Dale's signature "open" kitchen, a phenomenon the company takes credit for helping to create. At Dale's, customers could watch while chefs grilled their food behind—also a first—a large glass window. Birmingham diners wishing to experience the thrill of watching their food be prepared before their eyes these days can always visit the chef's counter at Chris Hastings' Hot and Hot Fish Club.

Another signature at Dale's was its "Gambler's Special": customers wouldn't know what cut of steak they were eating until it appeared in front of them on their plate. In the early days of the restaurant, diners could get a top sirloin steak served with tomato juice or soup, French-fried potatoes, Dale's Chefs Salad and tea or coffee, all for $3.75. Dale's Seasoning, really more of a liquid marinade that flavored the steaks, became so popular that

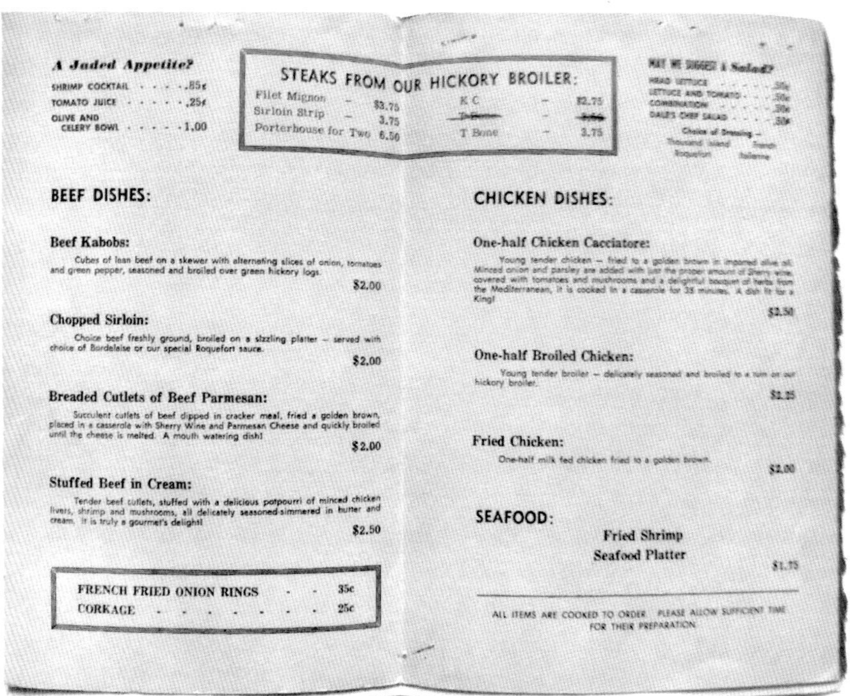

A Jaded Appetite?

SHRIMP COCKTAIL . . . . .85¢
TOMATO JUICE . . . . . .25¢
OLIVE AND CELERY BOWL 1.00

STEAKS FROM OUR HICKORY BROILER:

Filet Mignon	–	$3.75	K C	–	$2.75
Sirloin Strip	–	3.75	[illegible]	–	[illegible]
Porterhouse for Two		6.50	T Bone	–	3.75

MAY WE SUGGEST A Salad?

HEAD LETTUCE
LETTUCE AND TOMATO
COMBINATION
DALE'S CHEF SALAD

BEEF DISHES:

Beef Kabobs:
Cubes of lean beef on a skewer with alternating slices of onion, tomatoes and green pepper, seasoned and broiled over green hickory logs.
$2.00

Chopped Sirloin:
Choice beef freshly ground, broiled on a sizzling platter – served with choice of Bordelaise or our special Roquefort sauce.
$2.00

Breaded Cutlets of Beef Parmesan:
Succulent cutlets of beef dipped in cracker meal, fried a golden brown, placed in a casserole with Sherry Wine and Parmesan Cheese and quickly broiled until the cheese is melted. A mouth watering dish!
$2.00

Stuffed Beef in Cream:
Tender beef cutlets, stuffed with a delicious potpourri of minced chicken livers, shrimp and mushrooms, all delicately seasoned-simmered in butter and cream. It is truly a gourmet's delight!
$2.50

FRENCH FRIED ONION RINGS - - 35c
CORKAGE 25c

CHICKEN DISHES:

One-half Chicken Cacciatore:
Young tender chicken – fried to a golden brown in imported olive oil. Minced onion and parsley are added with just the proper amount of Sherry wine, covered with tomatoes and mushrooms and a delightful bouquet of herbs from the Mediterranean. It is cooked in a casserole for 35 minutes. A dish fit for a King!
$2.50

One-half Broiled Chicken:
Young tender broiler – delicately seasoned and broiled to a turn on our hickory broiler.
$2.25

Fried Chicken:
One-half milk fed chicken fried to a golden brown.
$2.00

SEAFOOD:

Fried Shrimp
Seafood Platter
$1.75

ALL ITEMS ARE COOKED TO ORDER. PLEASE ALLOW SUFFICIENT TIME FOR THEIR PREPARATION.

Dale's menu. *Courtesy of the Birmingham History Center; photograph by Emily Brown.*

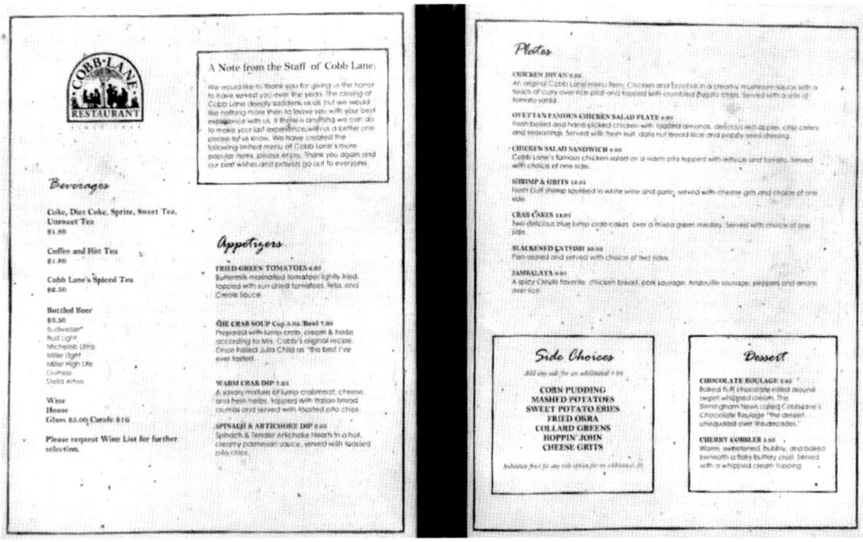

Cobb Lane Restaurant menu. *Courtesy of the Birmingham History Center; photograph by Emily Brown.*

customers would often ask for a bottle to take home, and the owners would have to fill a soft drink bottle in order to give it to them. So in 1975, the owners finally decided to standardize the recipe and bottling procedures so they could sell the seasoning.

Cobb Lane Restaurant, located in Southside on the street later renamed for the restaurant, became the go-to spot in the city for delicacies like she-crab soup and chocolate roulage. Virginia Cobb, who opened the restaurant in 1948, ran the business until she was in her eighties. After changing hands several times, and even changing names for a short while, the restaurant closed for good in 2009. But one of its last menus included the specialties that had made the restaurant a favorite over the years. The famed she-crab soup reportedly made Julia Child declare it the best she'd ever had, but the shaded courtyard adjacent to the small restaurant, where diners could enjoy the chicken divan amid the oaks, will be just as missed as the food.

Opened in 1951, The Club offered Birmingham patrons not only a chance to become members of a private club known for its service as much as its food but also the opportunity to enjoy panoramic views of the young city inside the striking, modern building or on one of its several large patios. The cantilevered roofs and parabolic shapes of the building were designed by architect John Davis (who also helped design Frank Stitt's restaurant

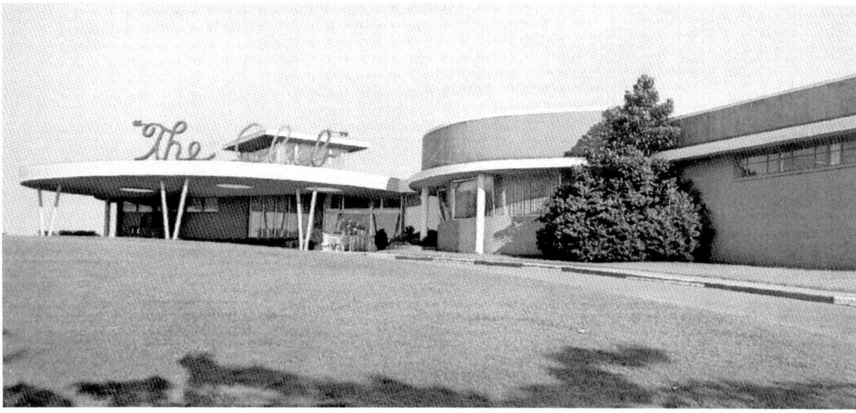

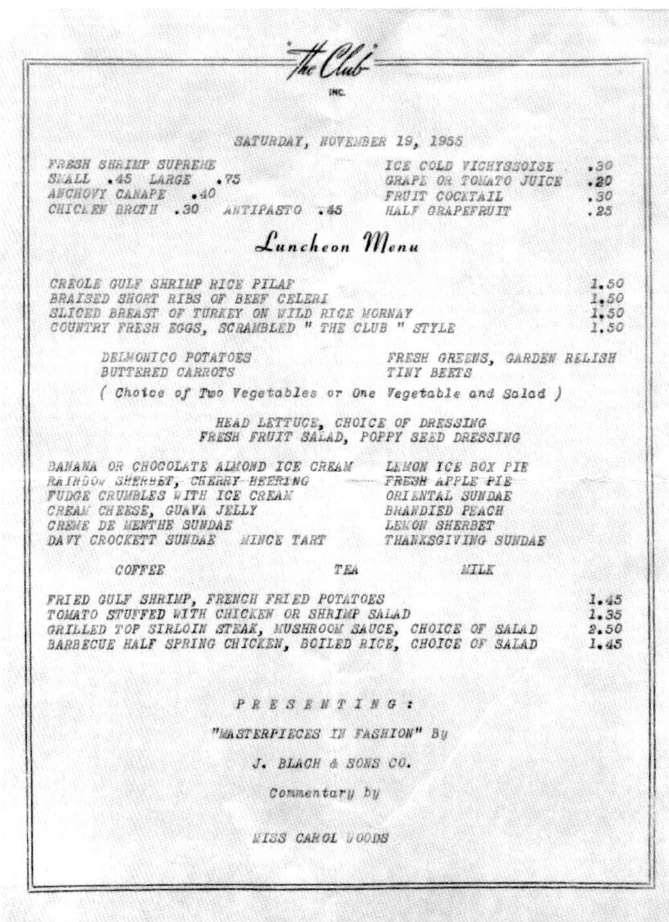

"The Club"
INC.

SATURDAY, NOVEMBER 19, 1955

FRESH SHRIMP SUPREME
SMALL .45 LARGE .75
ANCHOVY CANAPE .40
CHICKEN BROTH .30 ANTIPASTO .45

ICE COLD VICHYSSOISE .30
GRAPE OR TOMATO JUICE .20
FRUIT COCKTAIL .30
HALF GRAPEFRUIT .25

Luncheon Menu

CREOLE GULF SHRIMP RICE PILAF 1.50
BRAISED SHORT RIBS OF BEEF CELERI 1.50
SLICED BREAST OF TURKEY ON WILD RICE MORNAY 1.50
COUNTRY FRESH EGGS, SCRAMBLED " THE CLUB " STYLE 1.50

DELMONICO POTATOES
BUTTERED CARROTS

FRESH GREENS, GARDEN RELISH
TINY BEETS

(Choice of Two Vegetables or One Vegetable and Salad)

HEAD LETTUCE, CHOICE OF DRESSING
FRESH FRUIT SALAD, POPPY SEED DRESSING

BANANA OR CHOCOLATE ALMOND ICE CREAM
RAINBOW SHERBET, CHERRY HEERING
FUDGE CRUMBLES WITH ICE CREAM
CREAM CHEESE, GUAVA JELLY
CREME DE MENTHE SUNDAE
DAVY CROCKETT SUNDAE MINCE TART

LEMON ICE BOX PIE
FRESH APPLE PIE
ORIENTAL SUNDAE
BRANDIED PEACH
LEMON SHERBET
THANKSGIVING SUNDAE

COFFEE TEA MILK

FRIED GULF SHRIMP, FRENCH FRIED POTATOES 1.45
TOMATO STUFFED WITH CHICKEN OR SHRIMP SALAD 1.35
GRILLED TOP SIRLOIN STEAK, MUSHROOM SAUCE, CHOICE OF SALAD 2.50
BARBECUE HALF SPRING CHICKEN, BOILED RICE, CHOICE OF SALAD 1.45

P R E S E N T I N G :

"MASTERPIECES IN FASHION" By

J. BLACH & SONS CO.

Commentary by

MISS CAROL WOODS

Above: Postcard image of The Club's iconic architecture. *Courtesy of Steve Gilmer and What's on Second; photograph by Emily Brown.*

Left: The Club menu. *Courtesy of the Birmingham History Center; photograph by Emily Brown.*

Bottega) and can still be appreciated today, as can the iconic neon sign, but those orange rolls served at The Club hold a place much more dear in the hearts of Birmingham diners. A menu from a 1955 luncheon at The Club illustrates its luxurious style, offering appetizers from fresh shrimp to anchovy canapés and ice-cold vichyssoise alongside entrées of braised short ribs or sliced turkey breast with wild rice accompanied by fresh greens and a garden relish of "tiny beets." Dessert ranged from simple ice creams and pies to the exotic "Oriental Sundae," "Davy Crockett Sundae" and "Thanksgiving Sundae."

Italian Fare

At one point, Birmingham supported several authentic Italian restaurants at which diners could enjoy a romantic meal of pasta or veal with a bottle of wine. The heyday of these establishments, most run by Italian immigrants and their families, seems to have peaked in the 1980s, when at least three extremely popular restaurants existed downtown and on the outskirts of the city. It's unfortunate that none of these three—Lovoy's Restaurant on Green Springs, Romeo's Italian Restaurant on Seventh Avenue South and Rossi's Italian Cuisine on Twentieth Street—survived the boom of inexpensive, chain Italian-style restaurants, but these restaurants that celebrated family and tradition at least helped lay the groundwork for an appreciation of true Italian cuisine.

The first of the bunch, Lovoy's, opened in the 1960s and survived in its original location until the early 2000s, when it moved to the SoHo entertainment district in Homewood for a bit before closing for good. Lovoy's customers came to expect excellent seafood options, like the baked oysters on the half shell or Trout à la Gina, which was broiled in garlic butter and served on top of spaghetti with mushrooms and green peppers. The dim atmosphere was part of the restaurant's romantic charm, though it was also considered a family place. Veal Parmigiana, Lasagna, Spaghetti with Shrimp Sauce, and Chicken Cacciatore were also favorites.

Romeo's Italian Restaurant had the added romance of being located slightly below street level, so patrons had to climb down several steps to enter the restaurant with dark red walls decorated with Italian travel posters and lit by Chianti bottles stuffed with dripping candles atop iconic checkered tablecloths. George Sarris of the Fish Market Restaurant fondly remembers

Romeo's as one of his favorite spots to dine when he could get away from his own restaurant. "It was like a mom-and-pop store," he said. "You felt like you were a guest in their house, not in their store." Ernie and Herb Romeo ran the restaurant, but Mother Evelyn in the kitchen, cooking up her secret family recipes, was the restaurant's true draw. Pasta with meat sauce, clam sauce, butter and garlic or marinara were house specialties, as was the Eggplant Parmesan and veal served either piccanti or scallopine.

The interesting thing about Rossi's Italian was that it was actually run by a Greek man, Connie Kanakis, a partner of Michael Matsos's of Michael's Sirloin Room. The popular Broiled Snapper at Rossi's was served Italian style, with baked onion and tomato, to put its own spin on the specialty known in Greek restaurants around town. Various pasta dishes and well-liked Veal Piccanti and Veal Marsala rounded out the menu, along with traditional Italian desserts like cannoli and zabaglione. Rossi's served robust enough crowds on the weekends to require reservations. After this venture, Connie Kanakis went on to open his own namesake café at the Colonnade, which was well loved until it closed in the early 2000s, and he even worked with George Sarris at DoDiYos, a restaurant serving upscale Greek cuisine in SoHo in Homewood, for a time.

Joy Young's

One of the most interesting former Birmingham dining favorites, Joy Young's, remains the subject of many fond memories, even though the restaurant has been closed for over two decades. Opened in 1920 under the name King Joy, Joy Young's was notable not only because it was the first Chinese restaurant to open in Alabama but also because it offered Cantonese cooking alongside traditional southern dishes like fried chicken, which was named best in the city by the *Birmingham News* at one point.

Reported to be the first Chinese immigrants to settle in the state, Joy Young owners Mansion Joe, Loo Choy, Loo Bing and George Sai operated several locations in downtown Birmingham before settling into their famed location near the Tutwiler Hotel on Twentieth Street in 1925. From the beginning, the strangeness of dishes like egg fooyoung attracted Birmingham diners with a taste for adventure, and the restaurant soon gained a loyal following, perhaps in part because of the generosity of the owners during the Great Depression, when they served hungry diners even

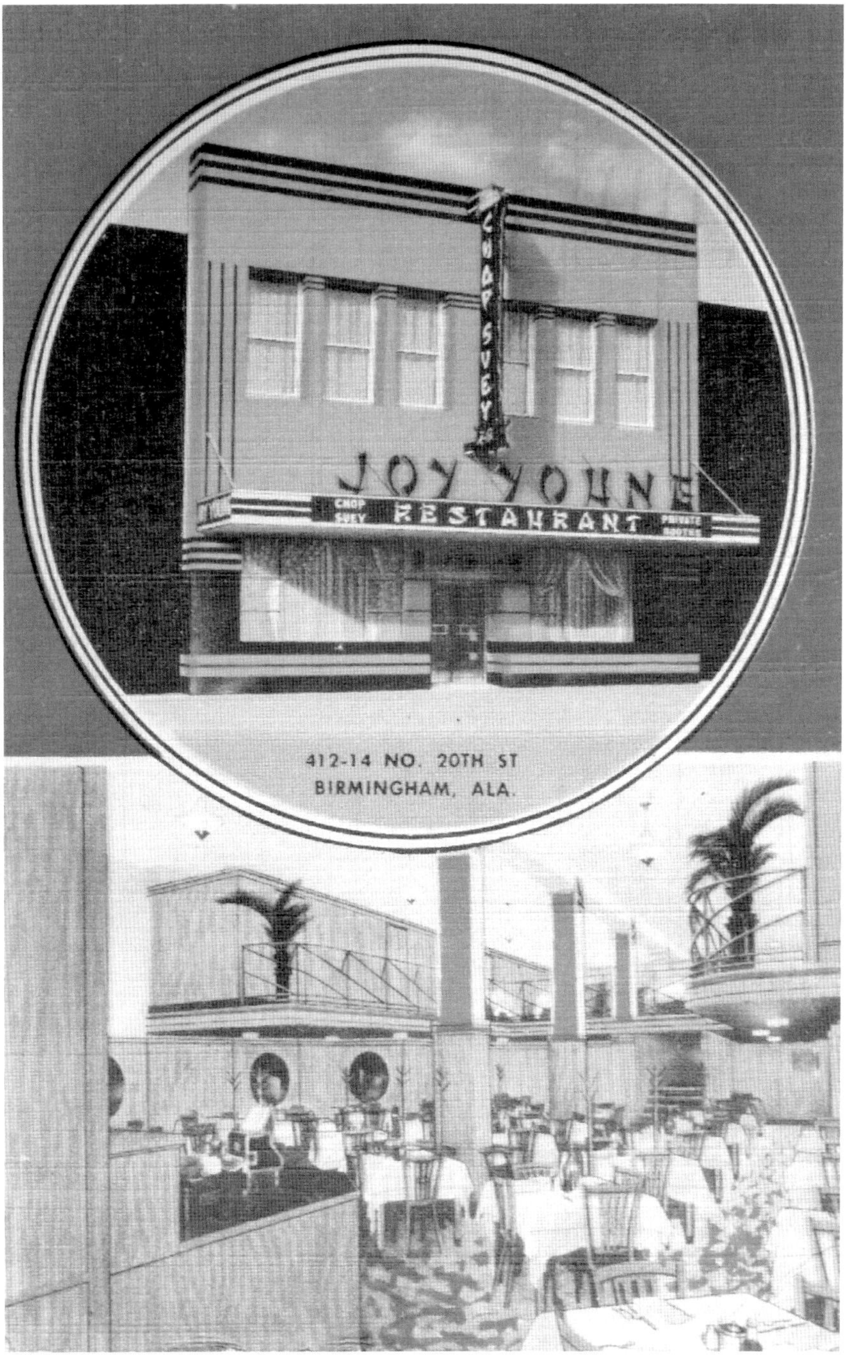

Postcard image of Joy Young Restaurant. *Courtesy of Steve Gilmer and What's on Second; photograph by Emily Brown.*

when money was scarce. Generations of Joe family members eventually became involved with the business, and customers remained loyal to the family and the restaurant over the years. This loyalty even defeated a Ku Klux Klan campaign to drive the immigrants out of the city, as customers refused to stop patronizing the restaurant.

Chef Frank Stitt remembers dining at Joy Young's and how memorable the meals always were. He said it was known as "a really good restaurant with exotic food, Cantonese food." As someone who has made his career by focusing on quality and hospitality, Chef Stitt also noted with admiration that "the family was very meticulous about their ingredients. The waiters had on white jackets. There were booths with curtains. It was a real dining experience, Joy Young's." Those curtained booths—where diners could enjoy private, romantic meals if they wished—were almost as famous as Joy Young's sought-after egg rolls.

Along with the egg rolls, which were stuffed with meat and vegetables and could almost be a meal in and of themselves, many varieties of chop suey with everything from asparagus tips to veal to beef and chicken liver filled the Joy Young's menu along with multiple styles of egg fooyoung, fried rice and chow mein noodles. Customers could also try imported Mandarin preserves, honey ginger preserves and fruits like "li chee" (lychee) nuts, if they so desired. When the crowds stopped coming downtown to dine, Joy Young's moved to a spot near Brookwood Hospital in 1980 to better serve its suburban-dwelling patrons. And though this location didn't last and the restaurant's move to Pelham in the 1990s precipitated its closing for good, Birmingham residents still seek the satisfaction of Joy Young's egg rolls. Supposedly Chop Suey Inn on Greensprings in Homewood sells egg rolls today that are as close as diners can hope to get to the historic ones.

5

BARBECUE

When it comes to barbecue, Birmingham has more than its fair share of options. Whether you prefer sandwiches or plates, traditional sides like slaw and potato salad or more modern accompaniments like organic cheese grits and sautéed local greens, there's a barbecue restaurant serving up what you want. Local franchises can be found in any corner of the city and surrounding suburbs, and loyalty to a particular brand can sometimes be passed down through generations, much like ownership of the restaurants themselves. Supposedly more than five hundred barbecue restaurants have opened in Birmingham since 1920, and though some remain only in the hearts and memories of residents, the new guys in town are earning reputations for seriously good meat.

Golden Rule

One particular brand of Birmingham barbecue grew from a small mom-and-pop establishment to a chain with popularity across the state. In 1891, in the community of Irondale just east of Birmingham, the Williams family opened a small barbecue joint named Golden Rule BBQ, a good stop on the road to Atlanta for travelers. They served pit barbecue, specializing in pork plates, but also sold beer and cigarettes and did the occasional automobile repair as years went on. In the 1930s, two Williams sisters still ran the business when one, named Ellene, married a man named Jabo Stone, an electrician who owned Stone Electric Company. Soon Ellene brought her husband in to help with the restaurant, and the two ran it together for almost forty years, serving the same pork plates and selling beer to the locals.

The Stones sold the original property and location of Golden Rule, with its dirt floor, shortly after taking ownership to move closer to the county line, a large spot with room for the family home behind the restaurant. This new location kept the dirt floor in the kitchen, but customers were invited to dine on the wooden floor spanning the walls of the dining room, much like a deck on top of the ground. With the expansion of Highway 78, Golden Rule moved again and took the opportunity to modernize equipment in the kitchen as well as add metal awnings and neon signs to help with visibility from the highway. With all these changes, it's no wonder the Stones spruced up the menu with the invention of their barbecue sandwich, which customers could order with chopped inside or outside meat or a mixture of both. The Stones ran Golden Rule when there were separate dining areas for whites and blacks, but they also ushered the business through desegregation in the 1960s.

Since Ellene and Jabo had no children of their own to pass on the business of the Golden Rule, when they were ready to retire in the late 1960s, Jabo began searching out a savvy businessman to whom to sell the restaurant, someone he could trust to keep Birmingham's oldest continually operating restaurant going. He'd become a fan of Michael's Sirloin Room and its proprietor Michael Matsos, so he approached him about buying the Golden Rule. Matsos eventually agreed, though he claims to have brokered their particular deal so that the Stones' only significant payment for the restaurant was a twenty-year royalty deal because he didn't want to pay anything for the restaurant. He joked that Jabo got the better end of that deal for sure. "Jabo Stone made lots more money than I anticipated paying on the royalty," Michael said, which must have hurt his pride a bit as a well-known sharp businessman. But Michael and his son, Charles, whom he eventually brought on to help run the business, made their own large successes with Golden Rule in franchising and selling the sauces. When the family sold a majority of the chain in 2009, there were almost twenty-five Golden Rule restaurants across the Southeast.

But back in 1969, when Michael Matsos first bought Golden Rule from the Stones, the restaurant had to move once again, this time due to construction of Interstate 20. This move was essentially across the street from the previous location, and the restaurant has been in the same spot for over thirty years now. The Matsoses pride themselves on selling the same pork plates and sandwiches, and this original location still sells Coke in glass bottles, something old-timers remember fondly. Michael made sure to keep the same style pit for cooking, though the current one is considerably larger than in the old days. "All the cooking is done right out there in front of the customer," Michael said. "And he knows what he's getting." Matsos put his own spin on Golden Rule though, aside from the expansion. He was responsible for bringing in chicken, ribs and beef brisket to the menu and even adding French fries as a side. Each type of meat has its own special sauce to go along with it. The original tomato-based sauce for the pork plate or sandwiches has changed only slightly from the days of the Williams and Stone families, and the Matsos family has added a sweeter sauce to better accompany ribs and chicken. They've even developed a mustard-based sauce for customers who might have grown up with a different style of barbecue and for franchises outside the state. These changes have helped with franchising, giving Golden Rule a universal appeal, and Michael credited his son, Charles, with being instrumental to the franchising idea and process.

These days, the Golden Rule does a booming business, even selling pies, such as the lemon icebox pie, made famous at Michael's Sirloin Room. The menu might have changed a lot from the days of pork plates and cigarettes; customers can enjoy a barbecue salad made with smoked chicken and honey mustard dressing if they're not up for one of Golden Rule's pork sandwiches smothered in thick barbecue sauce. And while variety might be good for business, attracting a wider range of customers, Michael knew the cornerstone of a successful restaurant is always good, friendly service. "The restaurant business as a whole is very difficult because you may have a good product, but if you don't have good service to go with it, you have nothing," he said. "I've always believed you can't compromise quality for a price. Quality comes first. That's been our motto, and I think we've been very good at it."

In an especially Birmingham-style twist of fate, Michael's son, Charles, who was the driving force in franchising Golden Rule and a savvy restaurateur in his own right, decided to open a hot dog restaurant in 2012: G-Dogs and Gyros. The idea came to Charles after eating hot dogs topped with his mother's special recipe for thick and tangy sauce with his mom and dad one day. Unfortunately, Michael Matsos passed away just a few weeks before his son's newest venture became a reality, but Charles said his dad was excited about the prospect of his casual restaurant serving their family's version of the historic Birmingham hot dog.

Ollie's

It's no secret that barbecue in Birmingham can spark controversy, even if the issues only arrive in the form of debate over sauce preferences. But one longtime Birmingham barbecue institution made national history in the 1960s for a different type of controversy, namely refusing to serve African Americans at its counters and tables even after the national civil rights movement successfully brought an end to the 1914 Birmingham law requiring racial segregation in public eating places. Ollie's Bar-B-Q in Southside put itself at the center of national discussion when it challenged the segregation law's repeal all the way to the U.S. Supreme Court—and lost.

Ollie's wasn't always such a den of contention, however, and had even been a favorite spot among African Americans and Caucasians alike. In 1926, James Ollie McClung, a former Merita Bread deliveryman (when it was delivered by horse-drawn carriages), opened Ollie's Bar-B-Q in a small wooden shack on Greensprings Highway. The original building sported a tar paper roof, plank floors and screens nailed in the windows, but the signature thin, vinegary sauce that topped trimmed, lean pork slow smoked over both hickory and charcoal for ten hours—a process that kept the original owners and cooks working through the night—drew crowds from the predominantly African American neighborhood in which the restaurant resided as well as from surrounding areas. The McClungs claimed the slow-cooking process, which encouraged any remaining fat in the meat to drip down onto the coals and further flavor the smoke, made their barbecue the "World's Best." The barbecue stand found such success that the McClungs had to expand in 1949 and again in 1959, passing the responsibilities of the restaurant down to a second and third generation.

In 1964, James Ollie's son and grandson Ollie Sr. and Ollie Jr. ran the business, closing on Sundays to show their conservative principles and placing signs on every table that read, "No profanity please. Ladies and children are usually present. We appreciate your cooperation." White customers made up the restaurant's base, and regulars could be served at the tables. But even after repeal of the restaurant segregation law, the McClungs continued to serve African Americans only takeout from the end of their counter. By the end of that year, the Ollie's case ended in the Supreme Court, where the law requiring that "all persons shall be entitled to the full and equal enjoyment of the goods, services, facilities, and privileges, advantages, and accommodations of any public place of accommodation…without discrimination or segregation on the ground of race, color, religion, or national origin" was upheld. A major victory for the civil rights movement, the ruling inspired Reverend Edward Gardner of the Alabama Christian Movement for Human Rights to remark, "There will be no more sit-ins, but from now on there will be walk-ins."

The McClungs and Ollie's Bar-B-Q complied and continued to change with the times. In 1968, when Interstate 65 was constructed right in the path of Ollie's, the barbecue place moved again, this time just a bit farther down Greensprings Highway to the memorable round building it occupied for the next thirty years. As Ollie Jr. took over more of the restaurant's operations, the restaurant saw changes to the original menu as well—though never to the original sauce. Barbecued chicken and barbecue salads were added to the menu that also included a seasonal mincemeat pie (with meat). In the early 1970s, the McClungs also began bottling and selling their sauce, which sold well at select locations. By 1999, Ollie's Bar-B-Q had moved once again, this time to the city of Pelham, about twenty minutes south of downtown Birmingham. The final incarnation of Ollie's lasted until only 2001, when declining sales and a lack of long-term interest by younger family members to maintain the business forced it to close. But despite the troubled history of Ollie's, the restaurant is still remembered fondly by many, as evidenced by the continued sales of its unique sauce.

Jim 'N Nick's

Nick Pihakis of Jim 'N Nick's Bar-B-Q has wanted to be in the restaurant business since he was fifteen years old. At age nineteen, he started working at Rossi's, one of Michael Matsos's establishments, and stayed there for the next eight years, learning the trade. By then his father, Jim, was ready to retire from his career in insurance and suggested they start a family business together. Nick jumped at the chance to join his father in living out his restaurant dream, and in 1985, they purchased a pizza franchise. The company's corporate headquarters decided not to allow transfer of the franchise and asked them to take down the signs, basically to cease and desist, which is when Nick and his father decided to try their hands at a southern tradition: barbecue. They hired a former cook from Ollie's to come and teach them everything he knew about cooking pit barbecue. Once they had their technique down, customers started coming in, though for the first few months the restaurant operated without a name or a sign. Nick said he and his father kept polling their customers, asking for suggestions for the new restaurant's name. Most suggested they name it after themselves since they were always around, and Jim 'N Nick's was born. Soon, they expanded to a second location in the Over-the-Mountain neighborhood of Riverchase in Hoover, and once suburbanites got a taste of Jim 'N Nick's delicious food, which they could easily enjoy at night and on the weekends, the restaurant's growth really began. As of 2014, there were thirty-four Jim 'N Nick's restaurants around the country, each owned in partnership with a local, and five more are expected to open in 2015.

Now Nick focuses on a business philosophy he calls "lateral service," which essentially means he believes in taking care of his employees, nurturing them, teaching them and helping them achieve their goals, which translates into good service and a good experience for the customers. Even with 3,500 employees, Nick still considers Jim 'N Nick's to be just a big family, and he believes in treating everyone as such. To him, barbecue has always been about family and sharing good food and good times with friends, forging those connections between people over a plate of food of which everyone involved can be proud.

Aside from cooking really great barbecued pork and smoked chicken with traditional sides like greens, macaroni and cheese and more, Jim 'N Nick's is famous for its addictive cheese biscuits. Each party gets a basket of these buttery mouthfuls served when it is seated, but customers often keep asking for more and often have to wait while a new batch comes out of the oven. Everything is done fresh at Jim 'N Nicks. The restaurants don't even have freezers. Nick says that when they hire people who have come from a chain restaurant background, they basically have to teach them how to cook. He has some quality help at his Southside location, however. Harry Pasisis, who ran Tom's Coney's hot dog stand from the 1950s to the 1980s, still comes in a few mornings a week to prep sauces and cheese biscuit batter and a few other things. Nick got to know Harry growing up in the Greek Church and said their families have been great friends ever since he can remember.

Though Nick didn't grow up in the restaurant business like a lot of second- and third-generation Greek immigrants in Birmingham, he does recognize the tradition he's continuing by owning such a successful restaurant business for almost thirty years. Jim Pihakis was the first generation of Pihakis men born in America, after his parents immigrated to Pennsylvania from Greece. His job in insurance transferred him to Birmingham, which is where Nick grew up, among a community of Greeks who were mainly in the produce, hot dog or restaurant business. Some, like Michael Matsos, even owned

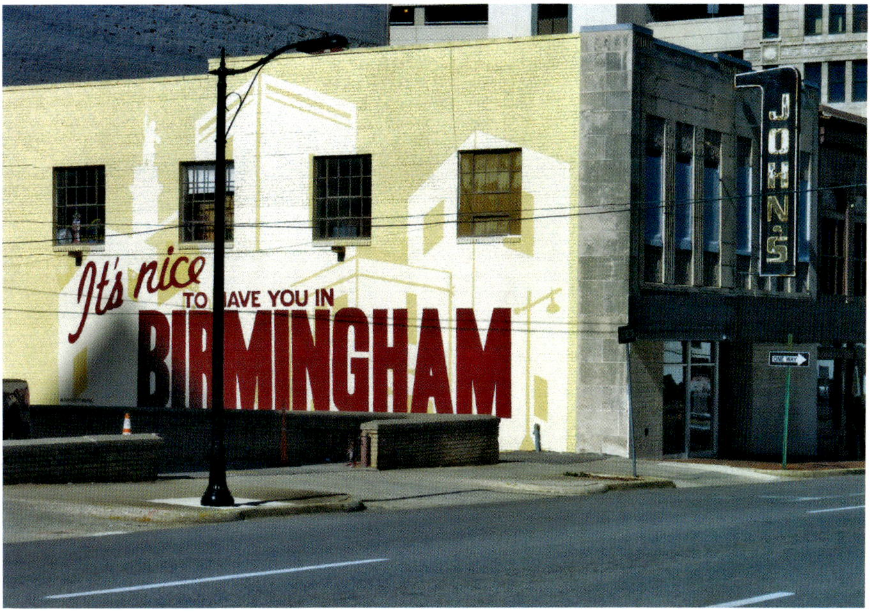

Outside John's City Diner in 2015. "It's Nice to Have You in Birmingham" mural courtesy of the Magic City Mural Collective. *Photograph by Emily Brown.*

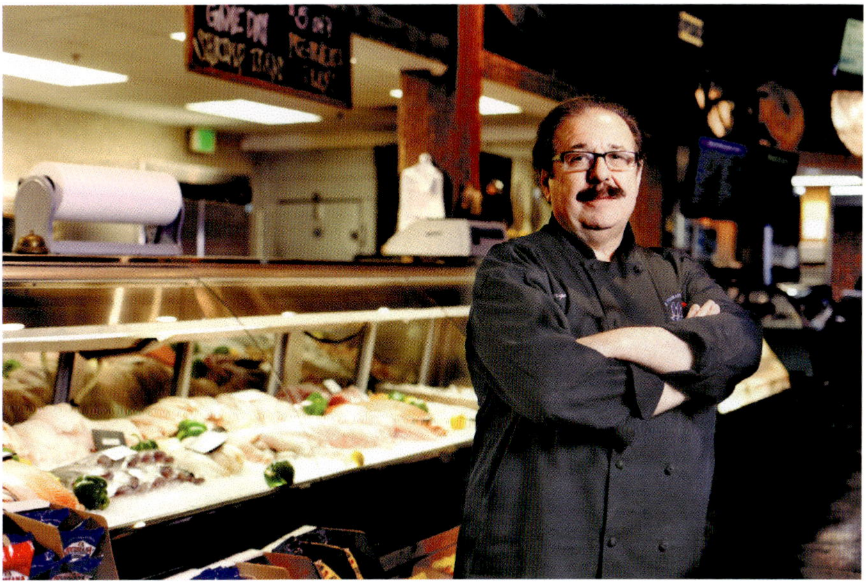

George Sarris near the fish counter in his Fish Market Restaurant. *Photograph by Arik Sokol.*

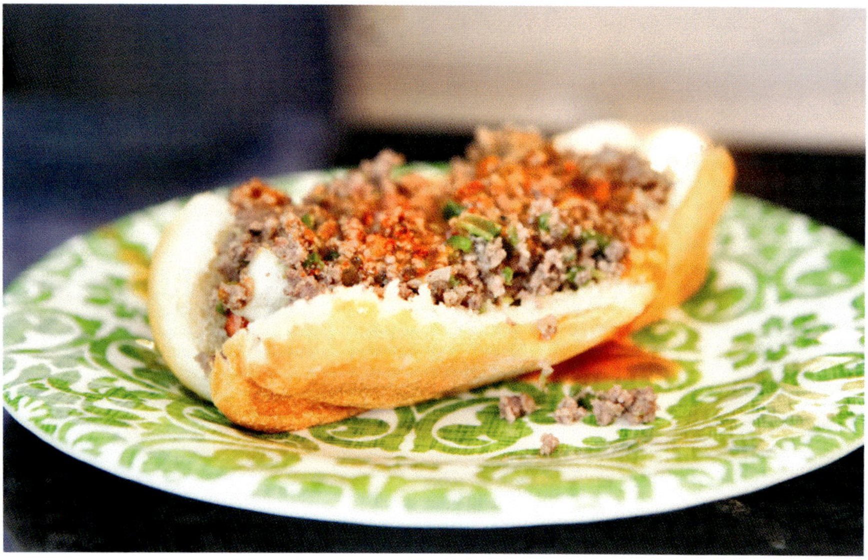

One of Tom's Coney's famous Specials, a hot dog with hot beef, cooked by Harry Pasisis. *Photograph by Arik Sokol.*

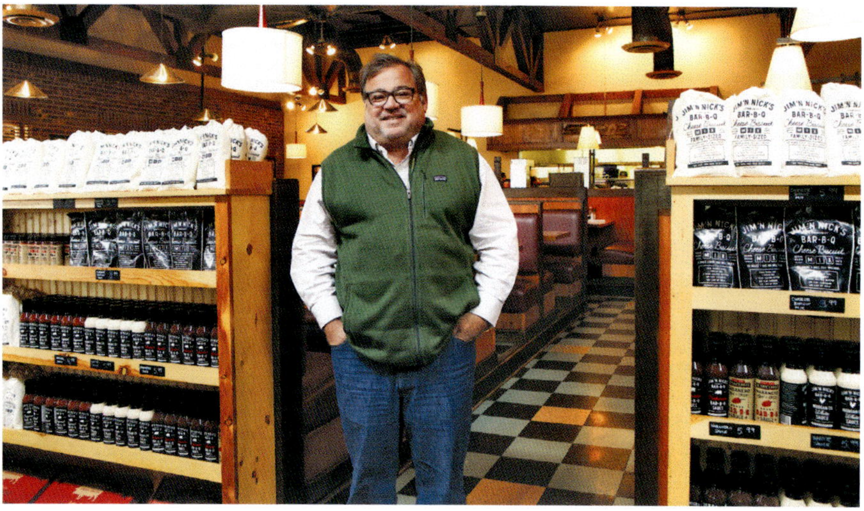

Nick Pihakis in his Greystone Jim 'N Nick's restaurant. *Photograph by Arik Sokol.*

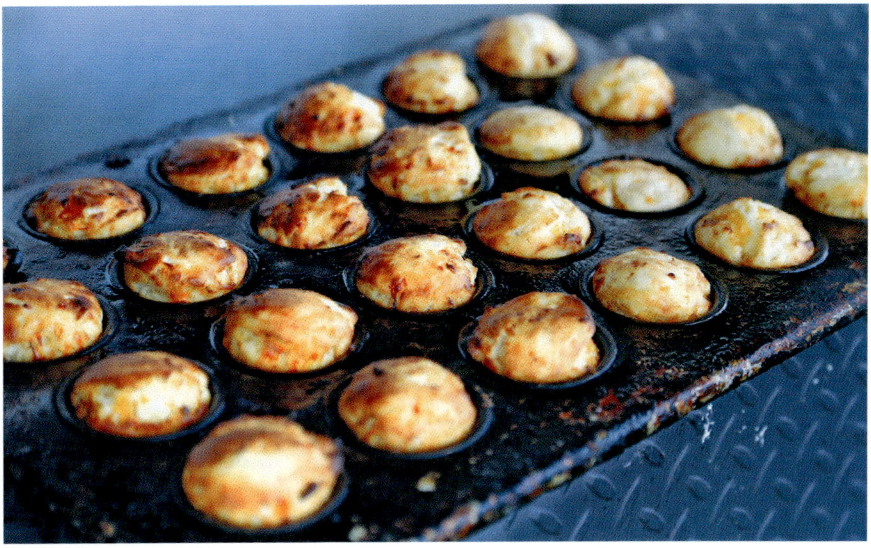

Jim 'N Nick's delectable cheese biscuits. *Courtesy of Jim 'N Nicks; photograph by Angie Mosier.*

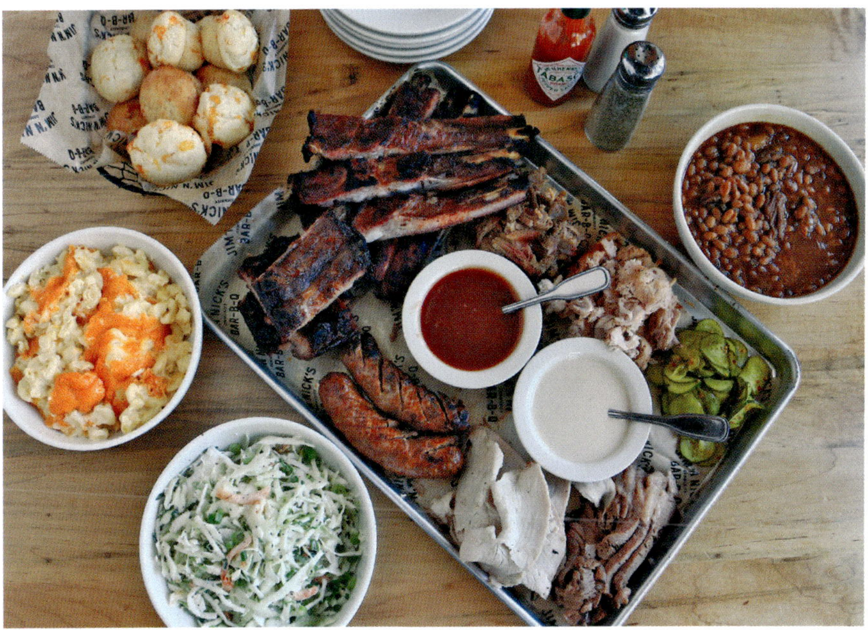

Mr. Jim's Deluxe Combo. *Courtesy of Jim 'N Nicks; photograph by Angie Mosier.*

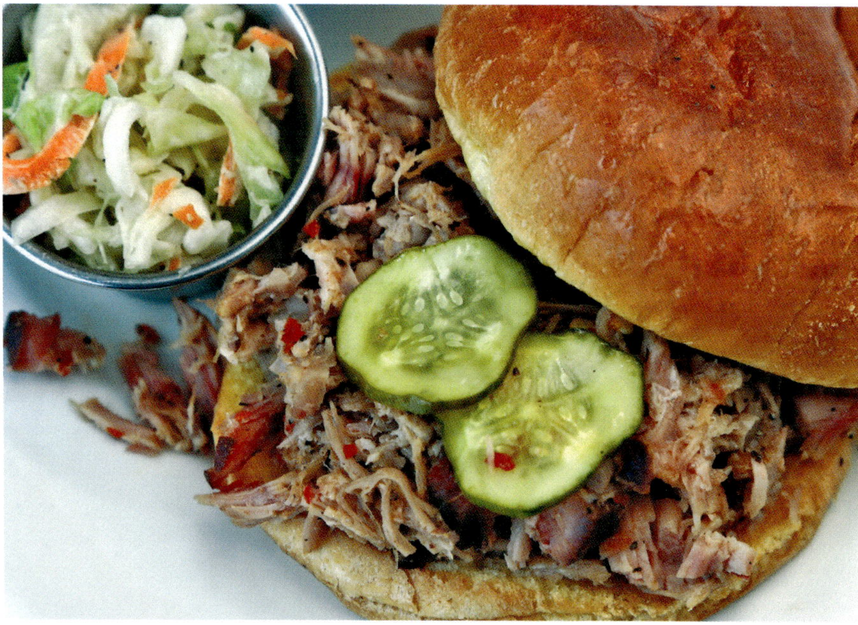

Carolina Sandwich. *Courtesy of Jim 'N Nicks; photograph by Angie Mosier.*

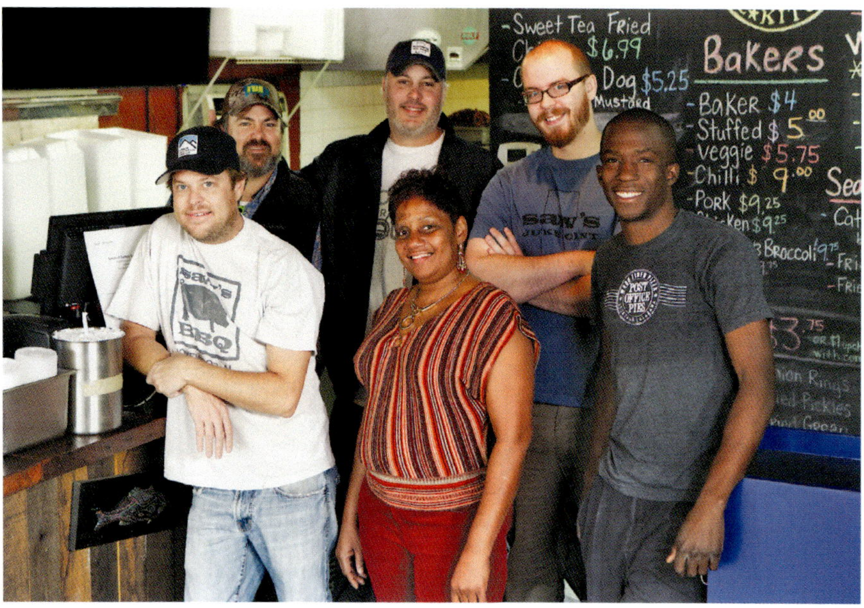

Mike Wilson (front, far left), owner of Saw's with partners (front row, left to right) Anastasia Nealey and John Hall and (back row, left to right) Michael Brandon, Brandon Cain and Randall Norman. *Photograph by Arik Sokol.*

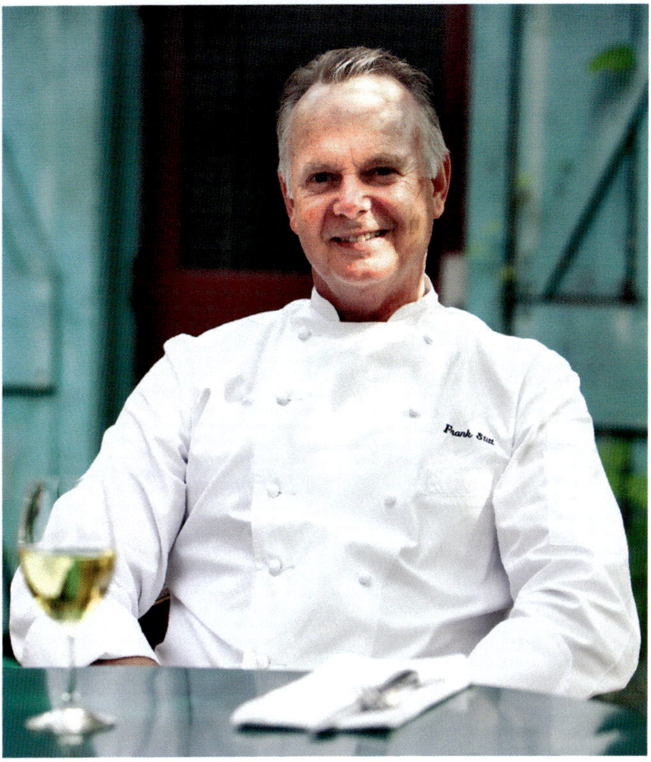

Chef Frank Stitt in the courtyard outside Highlands Bar and Grill and Chez Fonfon. *Photograph by Arik Sokol.*

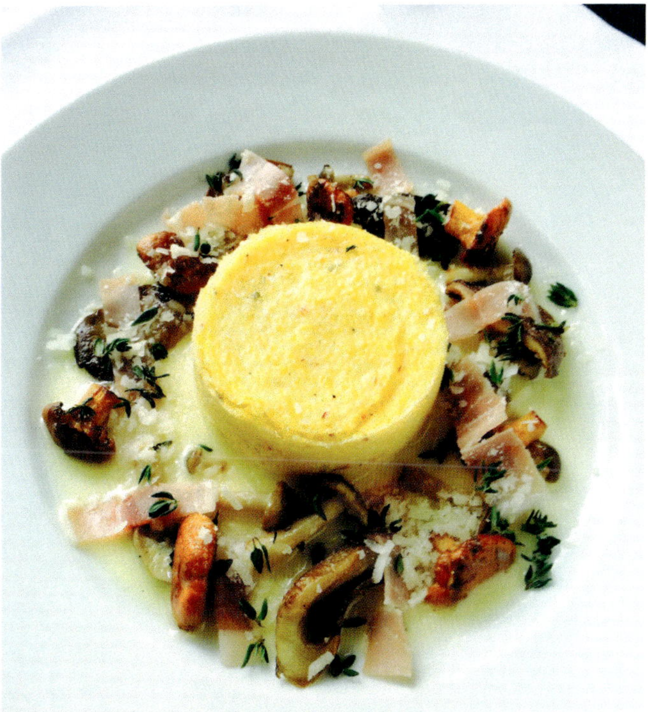

Highlands Bar and Grill's famous Baked Grits. *Courtesy of Highlands Bar and Grill.*

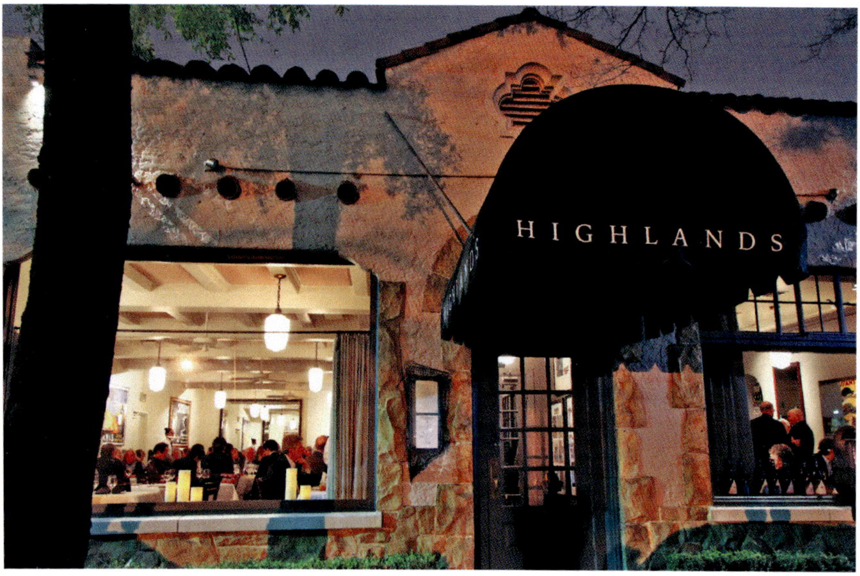

The historic architecture outside Highlands. *Courtesy of Highlands Bar and Grill; photograph by Marti Kilpatrick.*

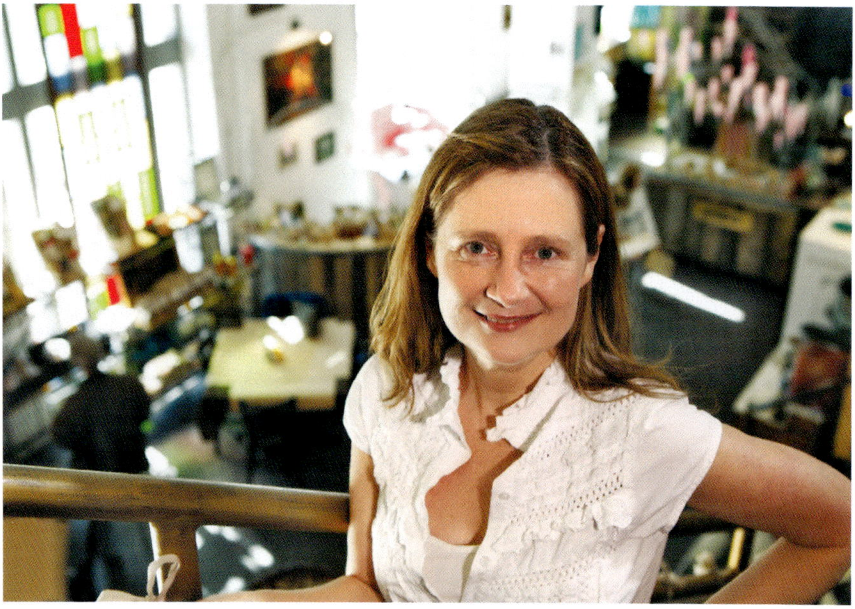

Carole Griffin on the stairs at the downtown location of her Continental Bakery. *Photograph by Arik Sokol.*

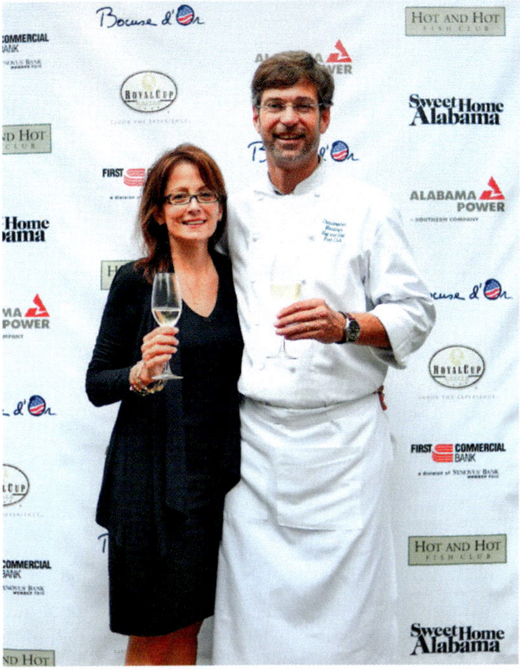

Chris and Idie Hastings at Step and Repeat Alabama Innovators. *Courtesy of Hot and Hot Fish Club; photograph by Bonjwing Lee.*

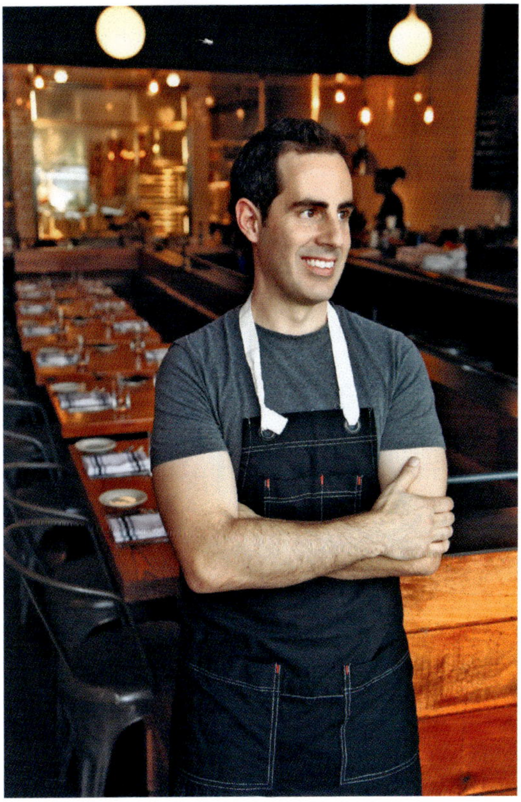

James Lewis, chef and owner at Bettola. *Courtesy of Bettola; photograph by Beau Gustafson.*

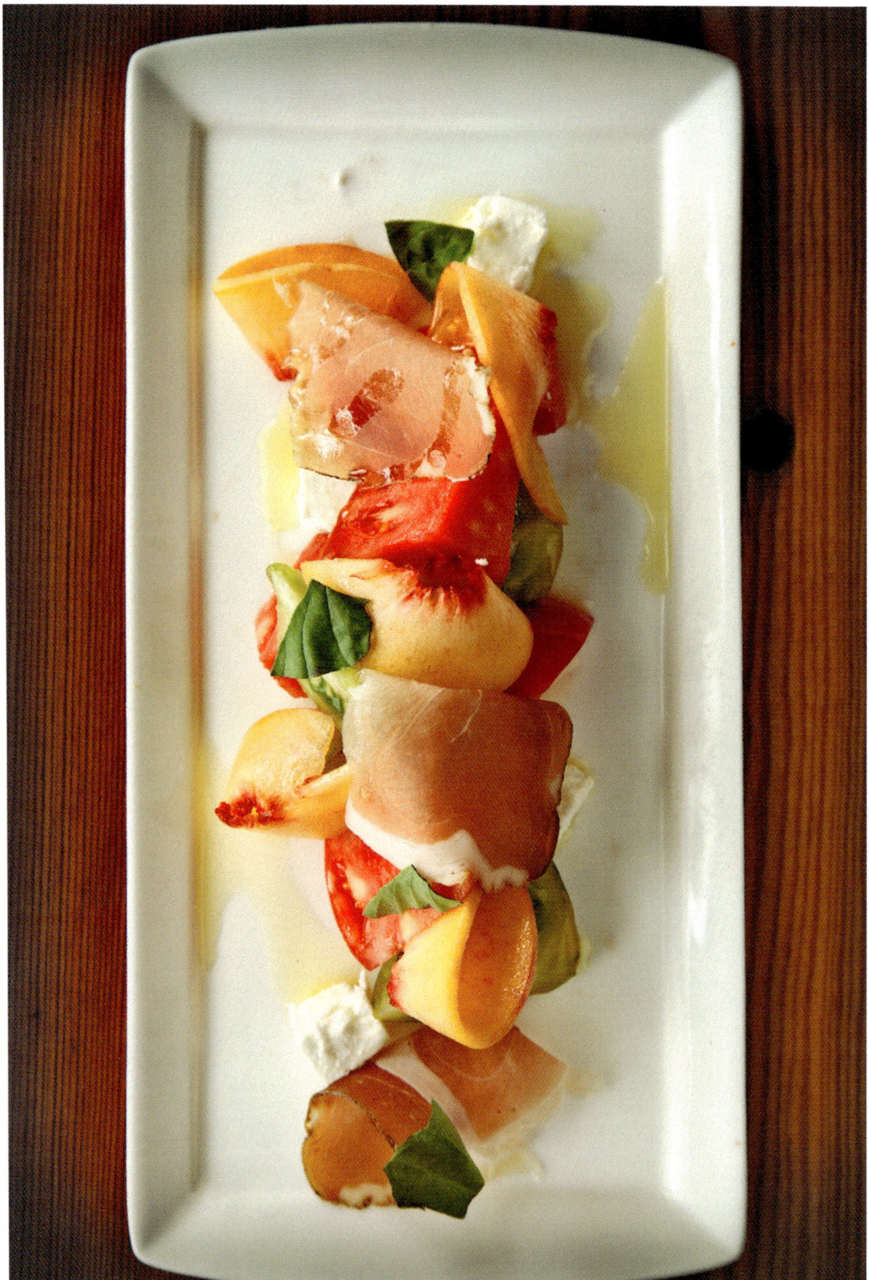

Dish with tomatoes and peaches. *Courtesy of Bettola; photograph by Beau Gustafson.*

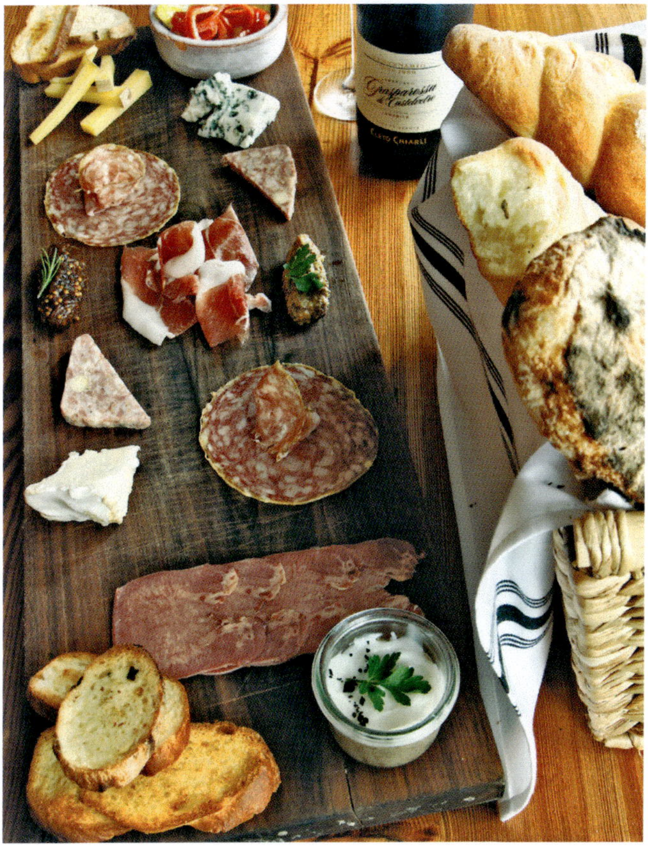

Charcuterie plate.
Courtesy of Bettola; photograph by Beau Gustafson.

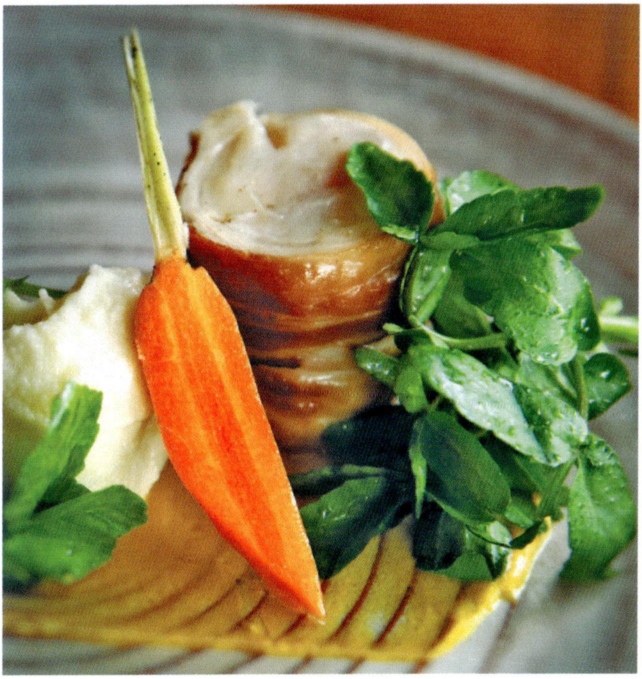

Dish with pork.
Courtesy of Bettola; photograph by Beau Gustafson.

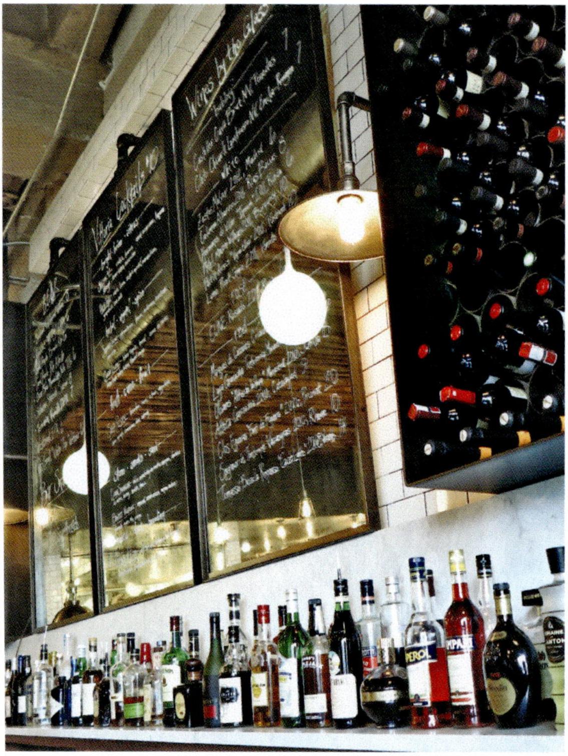

The bar at Bettola. *Courtesy of Bettola; photograph by Beau Gustafson.*

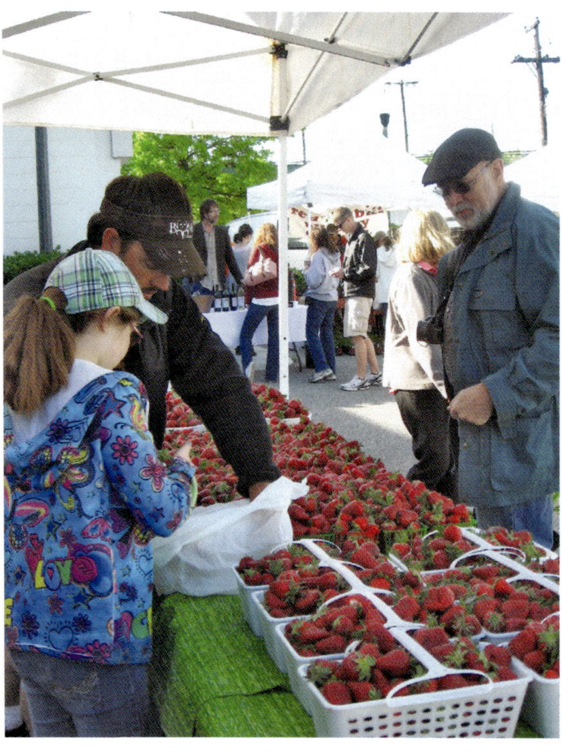

A farmer and his daughter sell strawberries. *Courtesy of Pepper Place Farmers' Market.*

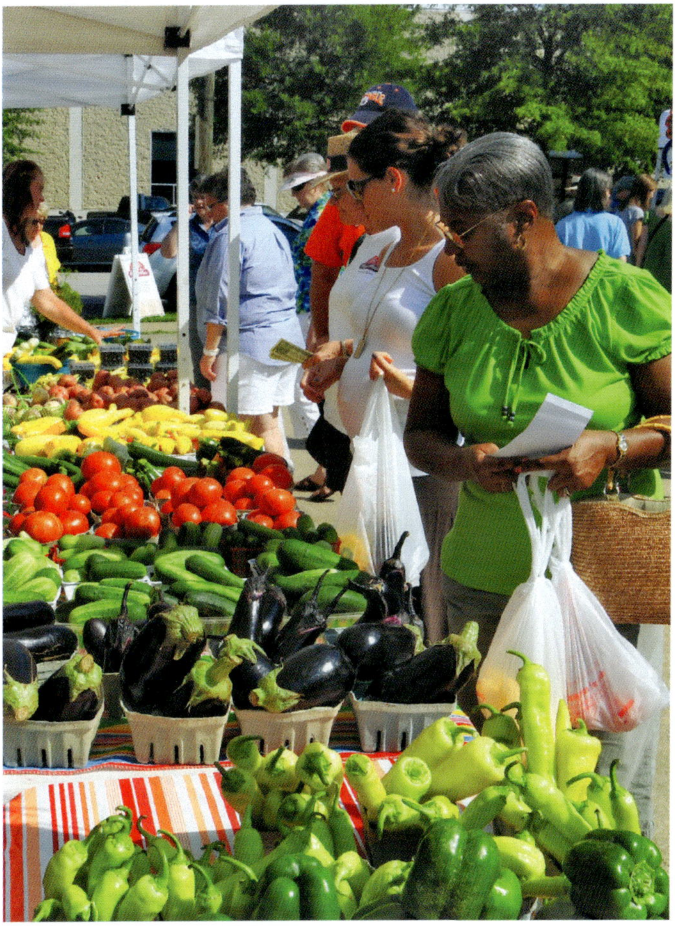

Right: Customers browse a rainbow-hued array of vegetables. *Courtesy of Pepper Place Farmers' Market.*

Below: The sun shines on the flourishing rows at Jones Valley Teaching Farm. *Courtesy of Jones Valley Teaching Farm; photograph by Cary Norton.*

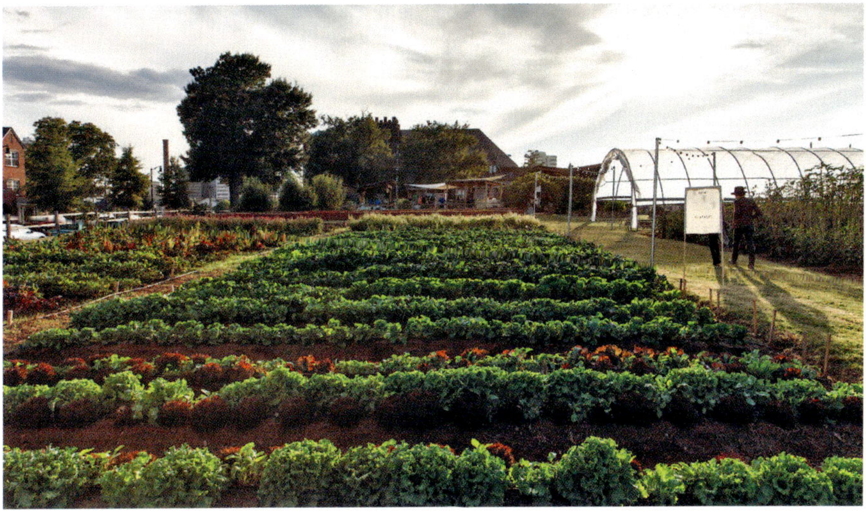

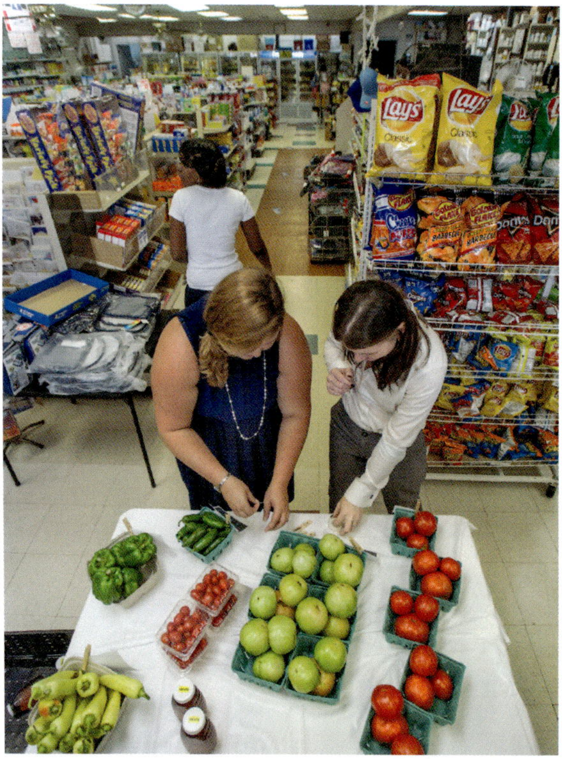

Left: Urban Food Project employees set out produce in a farm-to-corner store. *Photograph courtesy of Walt Stricklin for REV Birmingham's Urban Food Project.*

Below: An Urban Food Project famer displays his squash crop. *Photograph courtesy of Walt Stricklin for REV Birmingham's Urban Food Project.*

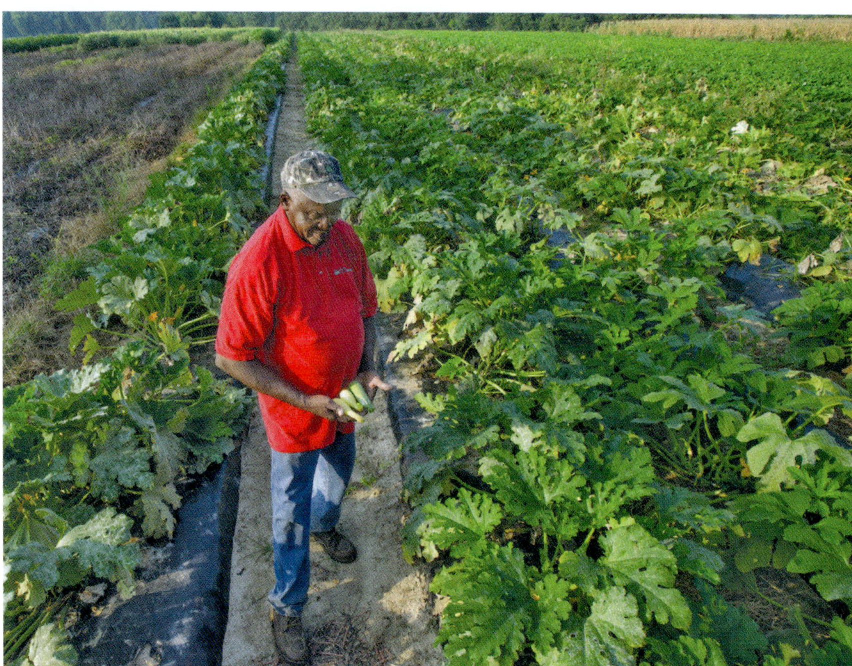

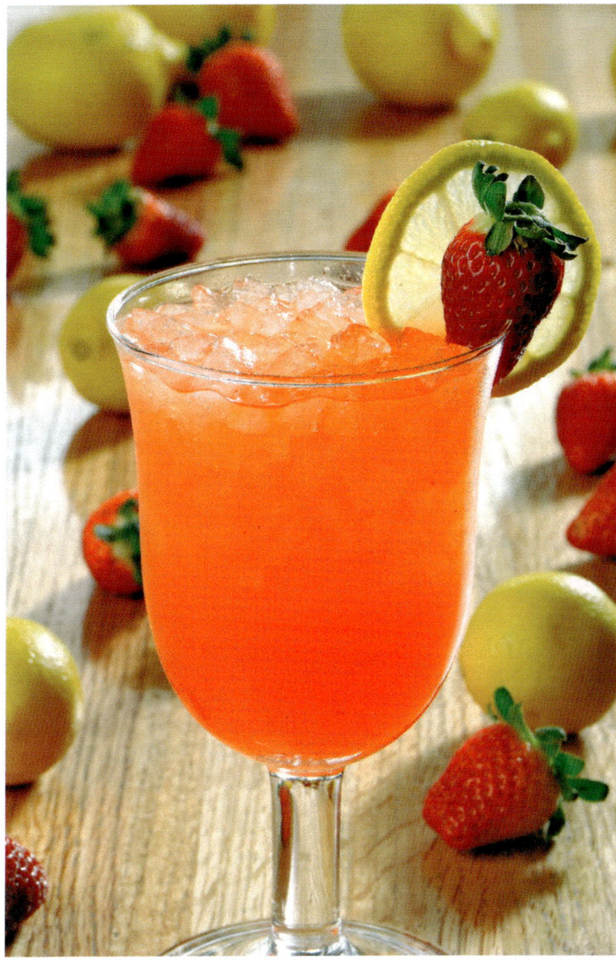

Right: Housemade strawberry lemonade. *Courtesy of Urban Cookhouse; photograph by Karim Shamsi-Basha.*

Below: Grilled Pineapple Ham with Hot Cheddar Pasta and Broccoli Salad. *Courtesy of Urban Cookhouse; photograph by Karim Shamsi-Basha.*

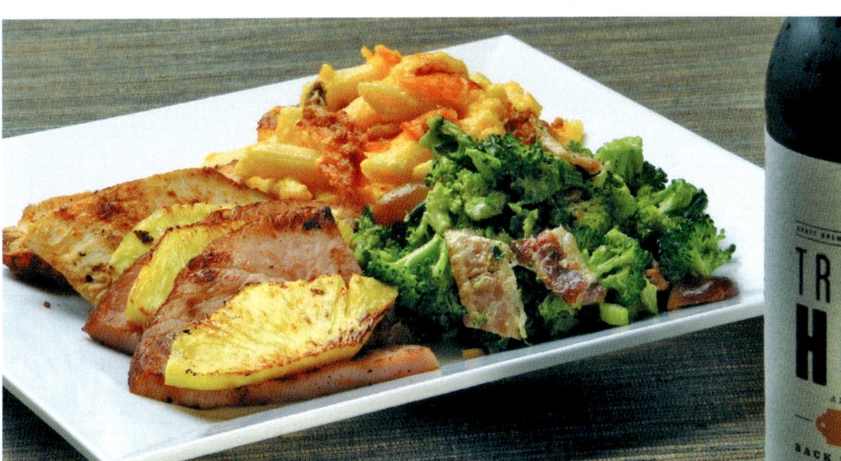

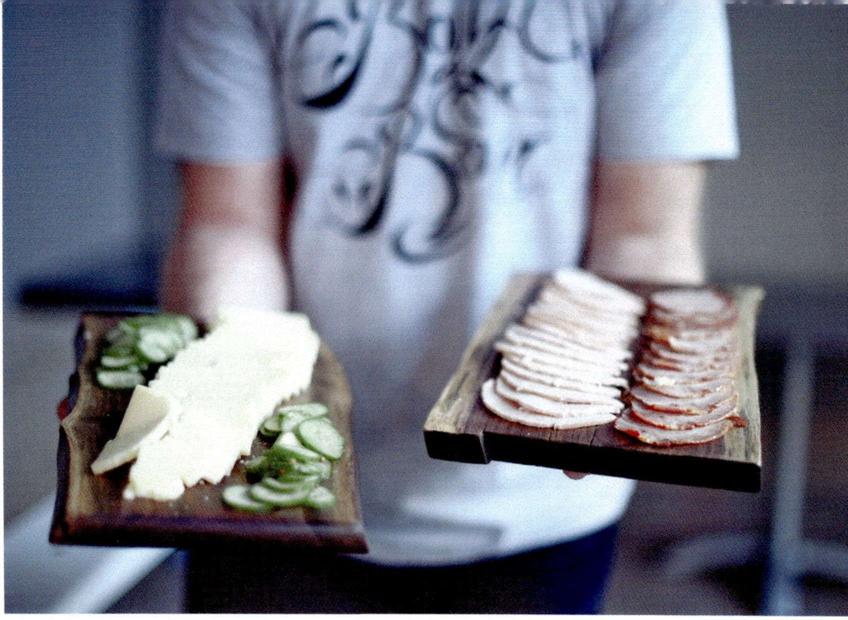

Bottle and Bone's cheese and charcuterie selections. *Courtesy of Bottle and Bone; photograph by Hilary Duke.*

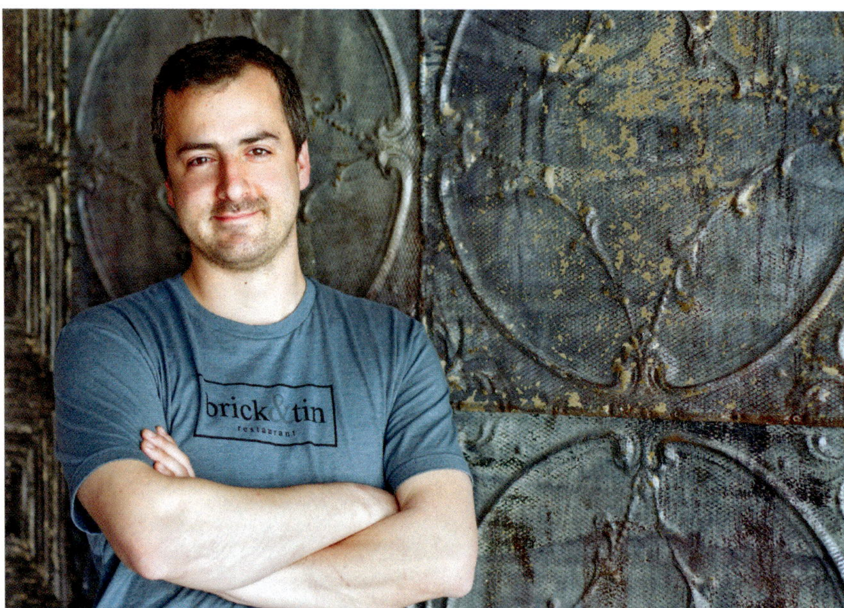

Mauricio Papapietro. *Courtesy of Brick and Tin; photograph by Graham Yelton.*

Opposite, top: The seasonal sandwich and salad with homemade bread and local produce at Brick and Tin. *Courtesy of Brick and Tin; photograph by Graham Yelton.*

Opposite, middle: The interior of Brick and Tin's Mountain Brook location. *Courtesy of Brick and Tin; photograph by Graham Yelton.*

Opposite, bottom: John Noles is ready to serve up burgers and pork belly buns from the Shindigs food truck. *Photograph by Arik Sokol.*

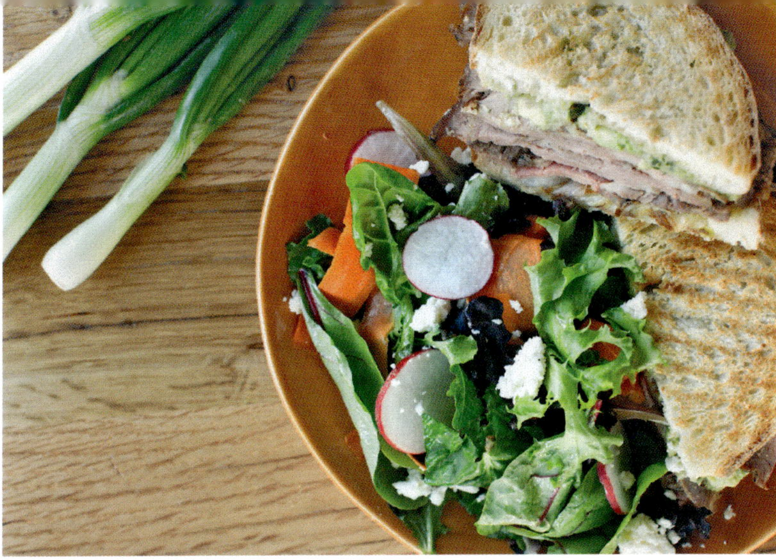

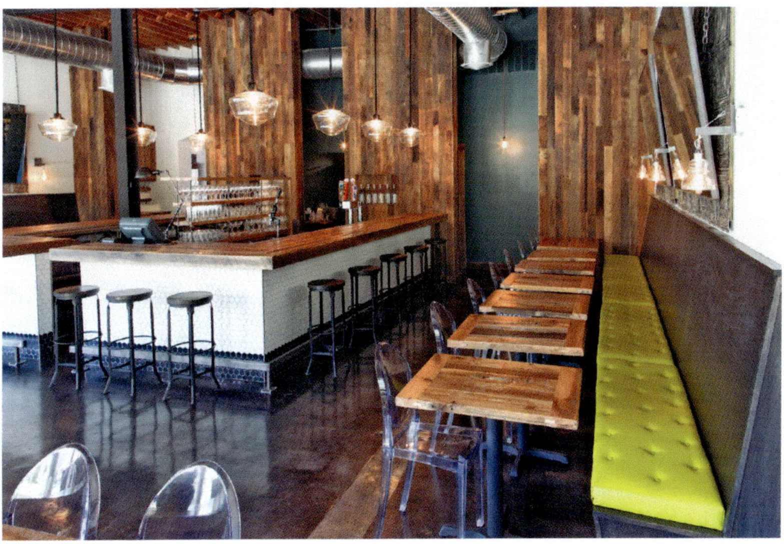

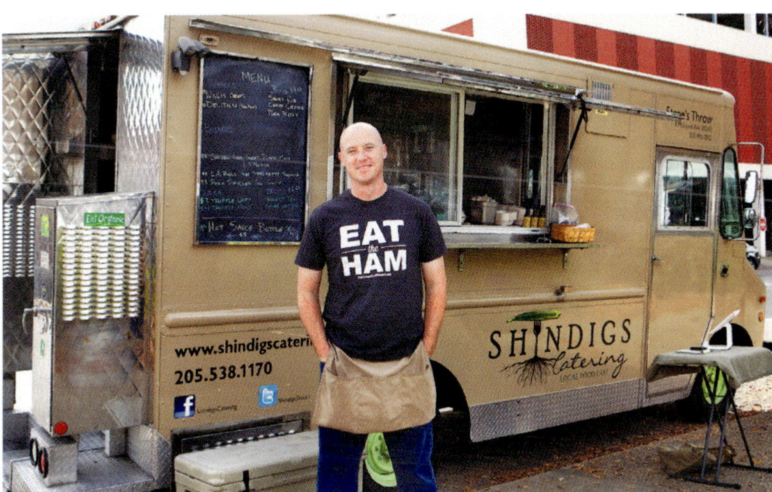
MENU
EAT
HAM
205.538.1170
SHINDIGS
Catering

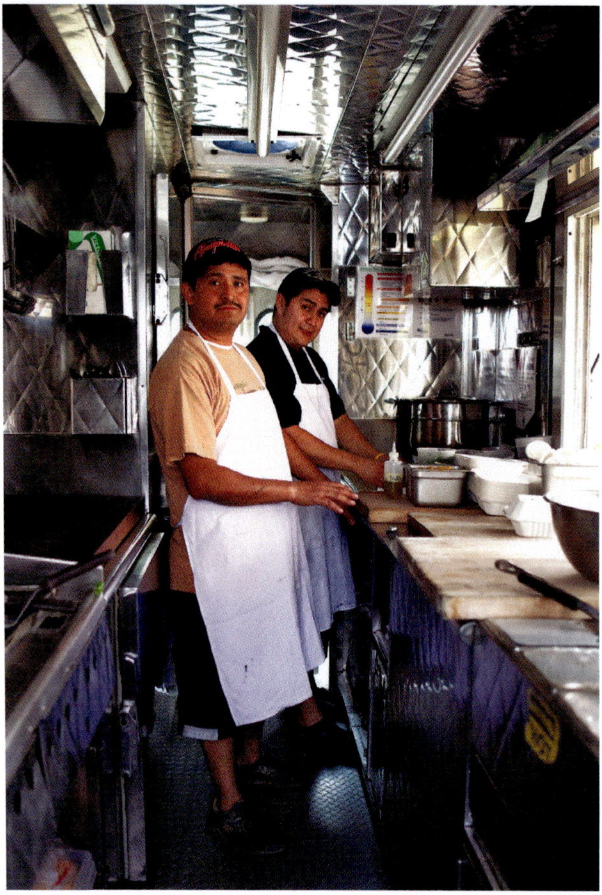

Hugo Artega and Louis Meza prep for the lunch crowd in the Shindigs food truck. *Photograph by Arik Sokol.*

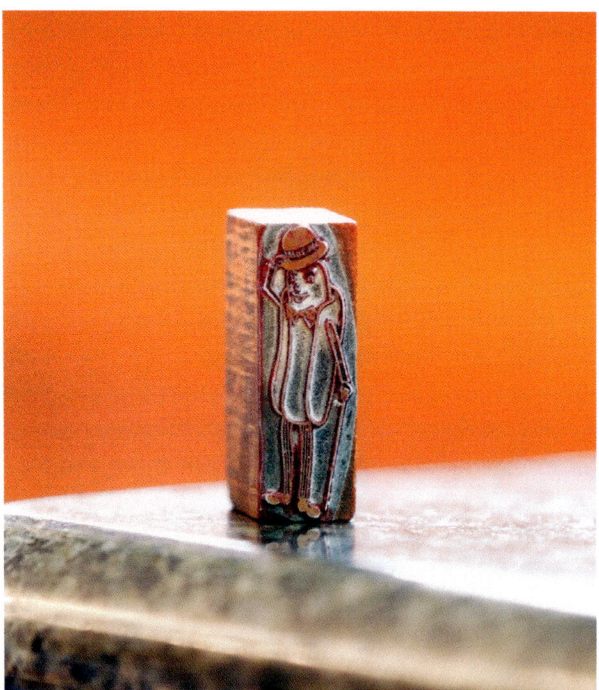

A stamp of the original Tom's Coney's logo. *Photograph by Arik Sokol.*

barbecue restaurants. "It's a wonderful food town. We got into it based on the fact that we knew it was something special," Nick said of opening the restaurant with his father. "It's about the experience more than it is just about the food. We connected with it. We understood it. I understood food."

In fostering a sense of personal pride in his employees and local owners, Nick has empowered them to give back to their own communities in meaningful ways. Part of Jim 'N Nick's agreement with its local owners is that at least 1 percent of sales will go to support community outreach programs. The company does not advertise, relying instead on these outreach programs focused in schools and churches and on teaching children and adults more about healthy eating to gain name recognition in each neighborhood. In Birmingham, Nick sits on the board at both Jones Valley Teaching Farm and Pepper Place Farmers' Market, two places dedicated to increasing the quality of and access to healthy food in our community, as well as educating people, whether through classes or cooking demonstrations, about better food choices. (Both organizations are covered in a later chapter.) "Our goal is to develop the next generation to be good servants to the community," Nick said.

As a companion to service and outreach, serving the best-quality food available is also at the core of Jim 'N Nick's philosophy. "We want to always use the best-quality food we can afford and buy local as much as we can," Nick said. Honesty in preparation and choosing the best recipes for its guests extends beyond the food served in Jim 'N Nick's restaurants, too. Since 2003, Nick and his restaurants have cultivated a close relationship with the Southern Foodways Alliance, a group dedicated to recording and preserving the history of southern foodways, a process that encourages conversation and a democratic atmosphere in which change and growth can come about. Through this relationship with the Southern Foodways Alliance, Nick and a group of other chefs, restaurateurs and writers have formed the Fatback Collective, an organization whose members come together to learn, share and help one another. The Fatback Collective has competed in the Memphis in May barbecue competition and also helped rebuild two barbecue restaurants that burned down, but its biggest enterprise of its brief existence has been the Fatback Pig Project. No longer satisfied with just serving the community through their restaurants, Nick and the Fatback Pig Project have purchased a pig-processing plant in northern Alabama to try to fill the gap left in pig farming and processing since Bryan Meats closed in Mississippi. They're trying to find a steady and sustainable market for farmers to grow heritage breed hogs. Then the plant processes the meat into things like bacon for Chef John Currence's Big Bad Breakfast, which opened a second location in Birmingham, and Donald Link's Cochon. The final goal for the group is to market its higher-quality product for wholesale. "We feel like we can carve a niche out," Nick said. "With our buying power, we felt like we could make a difference putting farmers back to work."

The fact that Birmingham is home to two distinct and successful barbecue chains with appeal beyond the state just proves that it's more than the food that makes customers loyal to a restaurant. With Jim 'N Nick's, the warmth and communal spirit honor the particularly southern spirit of hospitality while the focus on quality and sustainability for the future of hog farmers across the region brings the restaurants into the forefront of modern food concerns. Considering the first Jim 'N Nick's opened just a few short years after Frank Stitt began his crusade to make Birmingham a notable food town and the fact that Jim 'N Nick's has flourished for this long, the future of barbecue in Birmingham is in good hands.

Saw's

Speaking of the future of barbecue in Birmingham, one of the newest and most original and forward-thinking barbecue franchises around town still maintains a steadfast connection to traditional roots, even when it comes to its unique vinegar-based sauce. Since Mike Wilson first opened Saw's BBQ in Homewood in 2009, Birmingham residents have been clamoring for his pulled pork, smoked chicken, savory sauces and traditional sides, which is impressive in a market already known for lots of great barbecue. And with Mike's expansion into two other restaurants, Saw's Soul Kitchen and Saw's Juke Joint, plus a food truck, Saw's Street Kitchen, it's clear that Birmingham can't get enough of his artful and unpretentious food served with soul.

Mike came to Birmingham initially in 2000 to work in the test kitchens at *Cooking Light* magazine, one of the publications put out by Southern Progress in Birmingham. At the time, Birmingham was just beginning to see an awakening in terms of notable high-end cuisine, but there weren't a lot of non-chain, casual places to eat that still offered quality eats. In his native North Carolina, Mike had often spent weekends off from his job as sous chef at Dean and Deluca barbecuing with friends, experimenting with different cuts of meat, smoking times and eventually coming around to mixing his own rubs to season and color the meat. "I'm one of those guys trying to make everything homemade," Mike said. So eventually, he even developed his own sauces, which are vinegar based, like those from Ollie's were long ago. Once Mike came to work at *Cooking Light*, he still kept up his weekend hobby of smoking meat, and occasionally, he'd bring in leftovers to share with his co-workers. Word got out, friends raved and begged for more and Mike started thinking about finding a food truck so he could sell his barbecue more professionally at nights and on the weekends when he wasn't at the test kitchens. A photographer friend suggested a space in Homewood for Mike's commissary kitchen, something he'd need if he could find a food truck to purchase, but since it was so close to Broadway Barbecue, he balked, not wanting to step on anyone's toes. Mike did like the Broadway Barbecue space, though, and mentioned on a Thursday he'd be interested in buying it if the owner ever felt like selling. By the next Tuesday, the deal was done, for less money than it would have cost to start up a food truck, and Mike took two weeks off from *Cooking Light* to open his Saw's BBQ restaurant, keeping all the equipment from Broadway and even keeping on two employees, one of whom, Ms. Anna, runs the Homewood location still. By the end of those two weeks, Mike knew he couldn't return to his job at the magazine. The restaurant was an immediate success.

Saw's BBQ is small, like an old-school barbecue joint. Aside from the delicious meat, which Mike says stands out because he doesn't chop it, it's all pulled, customers enjoy traditional sides like greens, macaroni and cheese, corn, deviled eggs and more. The place felt immediately like it had been around forever and is warm and inviting with its close tables and smoky scent wafting to the street. "I try to take care of the little things and instill it in other people I work with," Mike said when asked why he thinks he had such immediate success. "You've got to take care of the little things, and the big things will come. It's all about the food, to me." He also takes pride in the fact that they serve the same ingredients, from the same places, that high-end restaurants around town use.

Mike's second location, Saw's Soul Kitchen in Avondale's newly vibrant neighborhood, came about just as much by chance. A friend suggested Mike meet Brandon Cain, a former chef de cuisine at Ocean who was ready to go out on his own in the restaurant business. They started talking with Coby Lake, one of the brothers who owns Avondale Brewing Company, an anchor in the neighborhood, and bought the spot with all the kitchen equipment and utensils almost the second they saw it, knowing it would be perfect for Mike's dream of a casual restaurant with great hamburgers and seafood sandwiches, plus his barbecue. The standout at Saw's Soul Kitchen, however, is the Pork and Greens. Perfectly seasoned and sauced pulled pork sits on top of a bed of cooked greens and creamy cheese grits, all topped with crispy, thin onion rings. When Alton Brown came to town in 2014, he raved about the ribs at Saw's. The third Saw's location, Saw's Juke Joint, opened in the Crestline neighborhood in 2012 and allows Mike and his partners Doug Smith and American Idol winner Taylor Hicks to combine the signature Saw's flavors with the atmosphere of a fun, neighborhood bar. The latest Saw's iteration is the food truck, serving a mobile version of customer favorites like huge, deliciously messy burgers and bringing Mike's restaurant dreams full circle back to a food truck.

Always on the move and looking for his next opportunity has helped Mike find spaces for new concepts and expansions of his brand at the right time, every time. His partnership in Post Office Pies, the new artisan pizza joint down the street from Avondale Brewing and the Soul Kitchen, has gained national attention for Birmingham and the restaurant's chef and partner John Hall. John Hall is a Birmingham native but spent time at Momofuku Ssam Bar in New York after culinary school. While in New York, John ran a bike-delivery pizza restaurant out of his apartment kitchen, and his love for crafting pizzas was born. Post Office Pies is a modern take on a classic, with toppings like house-made sausage and local vegetables on wood-fired crusts, but they keep a foothold in tradition with the restaurant's booths, which came from the old Michael's Sirloin Room. Within months of opening, Post Office Pies was named one of the top thirty-three pizza places in America by Thrillist.com, and Chef John Hall was featured in the *New York Times*, high praise indeed.

With hints that expansion into other states, in some form, is in the works for Mike, he's poised to become one of the more recognized chefs and restaurateurs from Birmingham. But his humble and grateful attitude makes Mike's successes well deserved. "Without the customer you don't have any of this," Mike said. "It's just about right and wrong. If you're not going to serve that plate to your mother, don't serve it to my guests." He believes in treating people right and treating people fair, from the customers to his staff. "You've got to be honored," Mike tells his staff. "These people worked hard for their money and are going to spend it on something we've created." Birmingham has definitely been welcoming to Mike, and he's grateful. "I'm thankful people in Birmingham embrace us and are adventurous…I think [Birmingham's] changing for the good, and it's only going to get better."

6
FRANK STITT AND QUALITY FINE DINING

A Birmingham Original

It's no exaggeration to say that Birmingham's restaurant scene would not be where it is today without Frank Stitt, the care he has taken in sourcing the best ingredients, the mentoring he has done for leagues of chefs and restaurateurs and the spotlight he has placed on hospitality as the key to memorable dining. Since he opened Highlands Bar and Grill on Eleventh Avenue South in 1982, the landscape of Birmingham dining has changed. Now, the variety of exceptional choices based on seasonal and local meats and produce can make where to dine an overwhelming decision. When patrons read over Chef Stitt's menus, they see not only an account of the incredible tastes they're about to experience but also a who's who of local farming, setting the scene for a very personal food experience. For over thirty years, Chef Stitt's influence on Birmingham dining has shaped the city into a place with bragging rights for its restaurant scene. He committed to sourcing local ingredients before the farm-to-table movement was even in the national lexicon, before the words heirloom and tomato were ever associated. Perhaps more than any other single chef, Frank Stitt's efforts to source and showcase the best that Alabama fields have to offer has pushed our city toward the booming restaurant culture we have today.

Growing up in 1950s Cullman, Alabama—less than an hour north of Birmingham—Chef Stitt spent a lot of time at his grandfather's farm, a place that still plowed the strawberry fields with mules and where chickens were raised for eggs to sell at local markets. Fresh, seasonal ingredients were just everyday food. He remembers making the drive to Birmingham to eat at the nice restaurants like John's, which, he said, "really did bring in good, fresh seafood" that he enjoyed with a side of slaw and cornbread. Chef Stitt also fondly remembers the exotic Joy Young's. "Their service was great," he said. He mentions Great Wall Chinese Restaurant on Valley Avenue as a place carrying on that tradition of "quality and excellence" in ethnic food. Another favorite from Birmingham's past (and present) was The Club, with its vast views of the city. "We would go and get dressed up and dance with my mom, order shrimp cocktail and lamb chops," Chef Stitt said. "There was a bit of a history of dining and fine dining being appreciated in Birmingham."

This appreciation for fine dining and connection to the land stayed with Chef Stitt as he began his chef training, working with such superstars as Alice Waters in her Berkley restaurant Chez Panisse and in Provence, France, with the food writer Richard Ulney, both of whom he credits with cementing his love of local and seasonal ingredient–inspired cooking. At Chez Panisse, Chef Stitt said he learned to "absorb their philosophy and their direction of working closely with farmers and purveyors" and shared in his fellow chef's excitement of doing something new each day, learning the history, both social and cultural, of each new dish they experimented with. Living in France gave him an appreciation for going to the market for ingredients for each day's meal. "That opened up my world," Chef Stitt said. "That connection between the farm and cooking reminded me of my grandparents' farm…The beauty of the French food, buying straight from the farmer on almost a daily basis, inspired me to want to come back to start a restaurant." In the beginning of Highlands Bar and Grill, whose menu features French cooking techniques combined with southern flavors, Chef Stitt spent a large portion of his time establishing relationships with farmers to help source his ingredients, mostly at the large farmers' market on Finley Avenue, where he met people who'd known his grandfather and his father, a doctor, back in Cullman. "That relationship with the farmer has been my ace in the hole as a chef and restaurateur," he said. Early challenges in "finding the guy who was the watermelon king, the guy who had the smallest okra, the guy who had good quality tomatoes" meant Chef Stitt had to work that much harder at creating his name and reputation in the business. "One of the dishes I wanted to do was this grits dish [which turned into his famous baked grits]. Everybody had bad quality commercial quick grits, so I would have to go to the health food store to buy organic stone ground grits. I found out the source after a while and started buying fifty- to one-hundred-pound sacks. It was constantly peeling the onion layers back, which I think is one of your main jobs as a chef," he said. Before opening Highlands, Chef Stitt notes that there were a few French restaurants "of marginal quality" around the city. "The thing had gotten to be a little bit more of fancy for fancy's sake and not necessarily quality of ingredients and passion for cooking and food," he said. "So, when I opened up, I think that I was one of the few chefs, proprietors, who would change the menu based totally on the quality of the ingredients, every day, and I think that was kind of a game changer.

In 1988, Chef Stitt opened his second restaurant, this time an Italian-inspired fine-dining establishment, Bottega. Housed in the left-hand side of a historic building on Highland Avenue, Bottega offers a different look into Chef Stitt's tastes, with homemade pastas and pizzas, fresh seafood risottos and Italian-style vegetables. Diners can enjoy their meals in the classical limestone building with its white marble accents and large leather banquettes. The building was originally commissioned in 1926 as a department store for Gus Meyer and was once headquarters to the Birmingham Area Boy Scouts. Etched with the iconic name "Bottega Favorita" above the front entrance, this Birmingham landmark was designed by William Warren, Eugene Knight and John Davis—the same architects who designed the Alabama Power Building downtown and who helped establish the city's look in many buildings from the early 1900s through the 1950s. The building was listed in the National Register of Historic Places in 1986. In 1990, Chef Stitt expanded Bottega to the right side of the building and opened Bottega Café, a more casual take on Italian. In 2000, Chef Stitt opened his fourth Birmingham restaurant, Chez Fonfon, a French-style café that features a one-hundred-year-old etched-glass door from Lyon and marble wainscoting and mahogany paneling around the bar that was reclaimed from a Birmingham office building. Fonfon serves French staples like steak tartare, escargot and moules et frites, but it is best known around town for its hamburger, topped with French cheese and served with crispy fries. The bar at Fonfon is the perfect place to people watch while waiting for a table, enjoying a Highlands martini or seasonal Pimm's cup with the quaint bar snack of pastel-hued soft-boiled eggs. When the weather is nice, Chez Fonfon patrons can also enjoy a game of boule in the back courtyard.

These four distinct restaurants are where Chef Stitt gets to reinterpret old traditions and create new dishes from whatever is fresh at the farm. "I really feel lucky to have these four different personalities of Fonfon, of Highlands, of Bottega, of Bottega Café, so I can kind of plug in this casual Italian or this

Italian that's a little more sophisticated and then this kind of southern with influences of France here and then this straight-up French bistro at Fonfon. I love those different personalities that allow me to explore," he said. And with these four distinct restaurants—something for every taste—it's no wonder his kitchens have sent out dozens of chefs into restaurants of their own, many maintaining roots in Birmingham and garnering the national praise that is making the city a foodie destination. Birmingham star chefs—such as Chris Hastings of Hot and Hot Fish Club, who once worked as chef de cuisine at Highlands; Clif Holt of Little Savannah, who previously worked at both Highlands and Chez Fonfon; Chris Newsome of Ollie Irene, who worked at Bottega, Bottega Café and Highlands; Chris Dupont of Café Dupont and Tau Poco, who worked at Highlands and Bottega; and Brian Somershield, who worked as chef de cuisine at Chez Fonfon and at Highlands, and Geoff Lockert, who worked at Chez Fonfon, both of Trattoria Centrale, El Barrio and Paramount—can claim lineage in the Chef Stitt family tree. As for his conscious role in this unofficial mentorship program, Chef Stitt said he thinks it's more a function of the longevity of his career. "I like to think that I try to build a team. Football was very important to me as a child, and I want to be a great coach, and I want to be a good leader. But I want to instill in people a core philosophy of respect and an appreciation for knowledge, for learning, pushing for excellence. So I think that some of the folks that have worked for me have perhaps learned from that and they've been able to embrace that in their own particular style. I think of Mauricio Papapietro [of] Brick and Tin and Brian Somershield as two really great examples of people. They were like kid brothers," he said.

With that team spirit and sense of family and community that Chef Stitt's kitchens inspire, as well as the food that consistently comes out of them, what makes Chef Stitt's restaurants notable is their level of service and hospitality. A large part of this hospitable and friendly atmosphere is due to the influence of Chef Stitt's wife and partner, Pardis. "She rarely gets the kind of recognition that she deserves," Chef Stitt said. "She obsesses about every little detail—where that spoon is, if all of the sugar is stacked up in the exact right way, how the napkin is placed. When you obsess about all those details there is something that happens beyond the sum of the parts that creates a magic in a restaurant. And that is certainly what Pardis does. I think that the level of sincerity and knowledge and graciousness of the service sets us further apart than a lot of restaurants." He also believes that the dedication of his servers, some of whom have been with him from the very beginning, make dining in his restaurants that much more enjoyable.

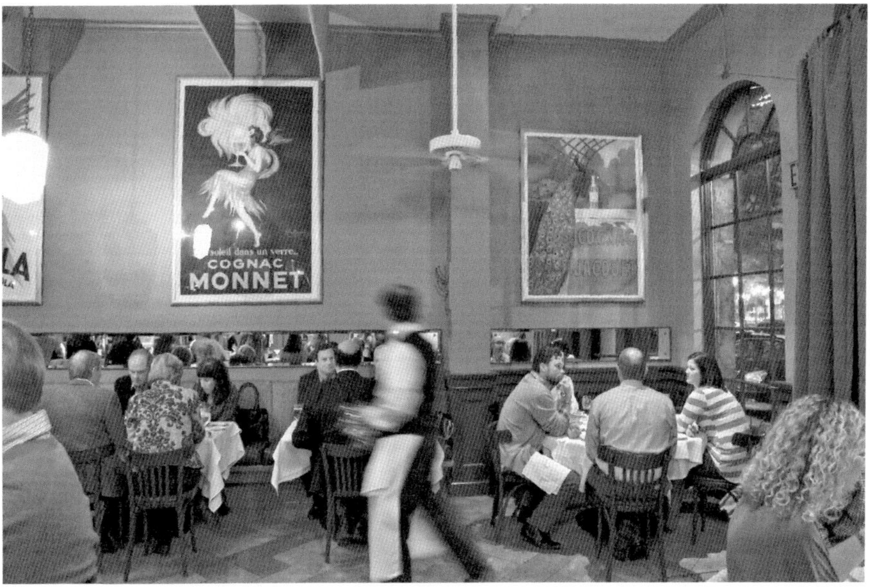

A typical busy night at Highlands. *Courtesy of Highlands Bar and Grill; photograph by Marti Kilpatrick.*

"These are great sales managers that understand psychology, that are articulate. They're knowledgeable. These are very important jobs," Chef Stitt said. "I wish that we could get the American public to respect that side of the restaurant business, so instead of being ashamed of saying, 'Well, yeah, I'm a server at one of the great restaurants in America,' you should be able to say that and be proud. Whereas as a cook you can kind of say that. When I started you couldn't."

On top of running his four restaurants, writing new menus daily and sourcing high-quality ingredients, Frank Stitt has been an important part of starting the Pepper Place Farmers' Market and the Southern Foodways Alliance, two groups that showcase and celebrate local food. In the beginnings of Pepper Place in 2000, Chef Stitt influenced the scene by talking to farmers and helping set up relationships between family farms and the market organizers:

> *I went over my ideas of some of the types of ingredients we wanted, types of spinach, types of beans and peas and corn and tomatoes. I kind of did a wish list, talking about how we'd like it to be organic. At that time, these guys were conventional farmers, with Edwin Marty who was just beginning*

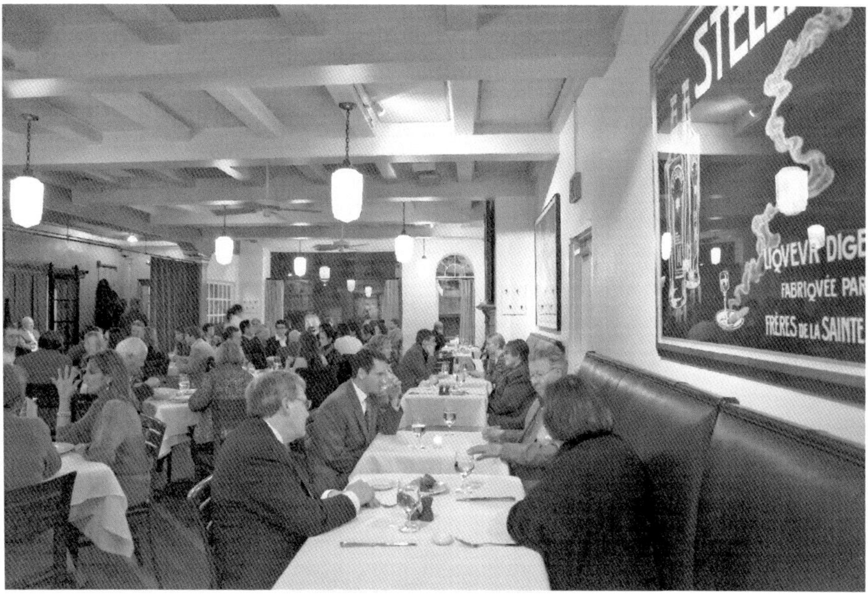

Patrons enjoying the elegant and comfortable atmosphere at Highlands. *Courtesy of Highlands Bar and Grill; photograph by Marti Kilpatrick.*

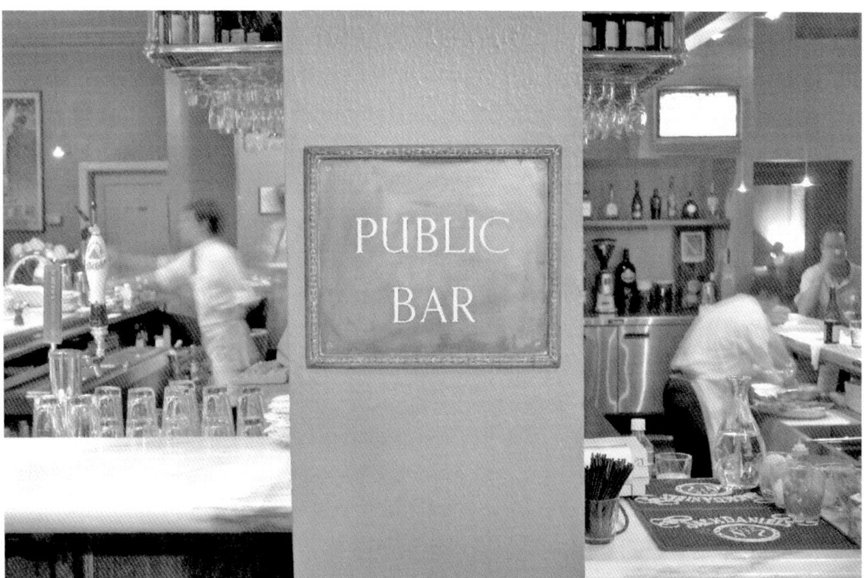

The bar at Highlands, a favorite gathering spot for locals. *Courtesy of Highlands Bar and Grill.*

> *Jones Valley Urban Farm and maybe David Snow and a couple others getting into organic farming, and we tried to support each other and tried to convince other people to grow sustainably and organically if possible. Most farmers were growing just a crop that they wanted money for. As a chef I started saying, "We want the best tasting tomato, maybe not the easiest to grow or to ship, we want the best tasting," which made some of the farmers revaluate the varieties they were growing.*

Farmers across the country were just beginning to rediscover heirloom varieties of plants and their unique flavors about this same time, creating a national movement toward specialized food production, so Chef Stitt was asking the right questions at the right time.

Sourcing ingredients is still one of the biggest jobs that Chef Stitt has, though now he has a solid network of farmers, foragers and purveyors who regularly stop in at his back door to sell their wares. "That's one of the things that I really try to keep up on is who's got the best ingredients and how can I get them and for a reasonable price," he said. He and Pardis also have their own farm, Paradise Farms, which supplies some of the ingredients for his restaurants. "We have incredible raised beds with everything from asparagus to edible flowers to carrots to all different colors of beets." But the relationships with local farmers like Michael Dean of Terra Preta Farm, who used to be a server in Chef Stitt's restaurants, and David Snow of Snow's Bend Farm will always be important to Chef Stitt's success. When Michael Dean shared his desire to start his own farm with Chef Stitt, he helped and encouraged him. "He's a wonderful farmer," Chef Stitt said. "He cares about the soil and the flavor and quality and taste." The ingredients he comes by through this support of local farmers, whether they are produce or meat, and foragers, who bring in items like wild watercress, mushrooms and purslane, keep Chef Stitt inspired in his menus. "That's how it was at Chez Panisse. That's how I learned to change my menu every day," he said.

Not only is Chef Stitt a truly nice guy—welcoming and gracious about the work his wife and staff contribute to his success, someone who still loves cooking for himself as much as he does visiting other restaurants as often as his busy schedule allows—but he's also seriously accredited in the world of food. The James Beard Foundation alone has nominated him for Best Chef, South four different years; named him winner of Best Chefs in America in 2001; nominated his cookbook for an award; nominated him for Outstanding Chef once and Outstanding Restaurant in America for multiple years; and named him a winner in Who's Who of Food and Beverages in America in

2011 and a Semi-Finalist for Most Outstanding Restaurant in America in 2012 and 2013. Chef Frank Stitt is a man who knows how to turn a field pea into a delicacy and is a true treasure for the city of Birmingham. His concern, however, and the impression he'd like his guests to take away with them is all about that connection to the land and quality ingredients. "I think that it has to do with respect for the land, for the farm, for the person who works the soil to create, to grow the great vegetables, to the person that's the rancher, the fishermen that care for the ingredients," Chef Stitt said. "I think that from that respect comes a philosophy of love and appreciation, and I think that philosophy of working to try to create just a little glimpse of beauty, of happiness in the philosophical sense, that's something that I'd like to pass on."

For Birmingham's culinary future, Chef Stitt would like to see more artisans entering the food business, people who truly care and have a passion for what they're growing, raising or selling. He cites great small butcher shops he's seen in places like Nashville, places where a customer can walk in to buy a quality cut of meat and have a conversation about how and where the animal was raised and what it was fed. Pepper Place Farmers' Market is another place Chef Stitt sees as the perfect avenue for these types of small businesses, continuing on from its current success. "We can have more of our farmers that are producing artisan products…frozen vegetables that are organically grown from someone that really cares about the soil," Chef Stitt said. "I would love to think that in corner cafés and restaurants, you would have locally sourced meat and vegetables. The individuality of people supporting their local entrepreneurs is really important. I think that Birmingham is in a good position to continue to expand. Great food doesn't have to be fancy, but you do have to have somebody that cares and does better than what they have to do."

Carole Griffin and Continental Bakery and Chez Lulu

Another Birmingham innovator, Carole Griffin, began her career in 1985 by opening an authentic French-style bakery in Mountain Brook. Though she grew up in Birmingham, Carole found her way to D.C. and worked at a newspaper job after college and traveling Europe, where she'd gained a strong appreciation for French cuisine and baking. A baker friend in D.C. shared Carole's dream of doing something more with her life, making something from scratch, and the two decided to come back to Birmingham to start a bakery with just $9,000. At the time, Carole saw Birmingham was becoming a place on the move, perhaps in part due to Frank Stitt's early influence, and with the opening of Continental Bakery and its artisanal French bread and southern butter rolls, she quickly became a part of that movement. A job as a night baker in college had given Carole both the skills for growing starters and the love for kneading dough, and she spent her time before opening learning the business side of baking. The small space she found for her bakery in English Village needed work, so Carole spent her startup money remodeling and refurbishing second-hand baking equipment. But her hard work and dedication to her craft paid off. "Within a month we were in the black and well supported by the local community," Carole said.

Restaurants still clamor for her breads, something that helped her grow her early popularity. But the honesty and artistry in the dough, combined with the quaint and welcoming atmosphere of the bakery, would have won over even the pickiest of clientele. By 1995, Carole was ready to expand her business, so next door to the bakery, she opened a small bistro, Chez Lulu, where patrons can enjoy tarts and quiches full of seasonal produce, soups like cool gazpacho in the summer and warming garlic soup in the cooler months, salads and more. Both Continental Bakery and Chez Lulu have always made a point to use local ingredients as well as sustainably raised meat and eggs as much as possible, practices that have endeared them to the community and made them a treasured part of Birmingham culture for decades.

Like Frank Stitt, Carole had difficulties sourcing quality and sustainable ingredients when she first began. "We used to give people bread for a handful of basil. We had a source for chestnuts for our chestnut soup. People would bring in buckets of figs for our fig tart," Carole said. "We did stuff like that, and we didn't even market it or talk about it because it was something we believed in and how we wanted to do business, but now it's something people recognize. It used to just feel like it was something that was important to us, but now our customers are requesting it, and that's wonderfully fulfilling." Through the years, Carole has developed reliable relationships with several farmers, such as Frank McEwen, with his organic stone-ground grits, and Michael Dean of Terra Preta. One of Carole's general managers even began raising chickens to help keep up with the bakery and restaurant's incredible demand for sustainably raised eggs. The bread itself, specifically Carole's very delicious sourdough, is the most local product offered, however. "It relies on a Birmingham-specific strain of yeast," Carole said. "This bread cannot be produced anywhere else in the world. Every bread has its own local character. Our sourdough is a Birmingham original."

Since Carole began in the 1980s, and with her help, Birmingham has come a long way, especially when it comes to sourcing the great ingredients that inspire her creativity in bread and food. "We were on our own and not part of a community," Carole said of her early days. "And now we feel like we're in the middle of a movement, surrounded by likeminded, kindred spirits. It's the best feeling in the world." Part of that movement is taking place in the heart of downtown, where Carole opened a second Continental Bakery location on Fourth Avenue North and Nineteenth Street in early 2014, the previous site of Mix Bakery. Just like the joint businesses in Mountain Brook, Continental Bakery Downtown offers fresh, quality food and baked goods in an inviting, eclectic atmosphere. Walking into either location feels a bit like walking into the living room of a European artist, albeit one who is particularly talented in the kitchen as well.

Chris Dupont and Café Dupont and Tau Poco

One of the other pioneers of Birmingham food, Chris Dupont, deserves recognition not only for his food, which artfully showcases seasonal and local flavors, but also for his trailblazing decision to purchase and renovate a building downtown for his restaurant, Café Dupont, before any other high-end chefs, bartenders or restaurateurs attempted to drive traffic in that direction. Really, enough cannot be said for the vision and bravery it took to open a restaurant downtown in the early part of the 2000s, and it's doubtful Birmingham would have the growing and exciting food and bar scene it does downtown today without Chef Chris Dupont's contribution.

Growing up in New Orleans, Chef Dupont was always surrounded by good food. At the time, New Orleans was only known for its regional and Cajun cuisine, and tourists flooded the city year-round for a taste of delicacies like blackened fish, turtle soup, gumbo and more. Chef Dupont worked in the restaurant business from the time he started taking summer jobs as a young teenager and jokes that he wasn't a very good busboy when he started, perhaps due to a lack of motivation. But when his bosses moved him to the back of the house, first filling water glasses for wait assistants and eventually graduating to working the escargot station, he found the inspiration he'd been looking for to do a good job. After coming to Birmingham-Southern

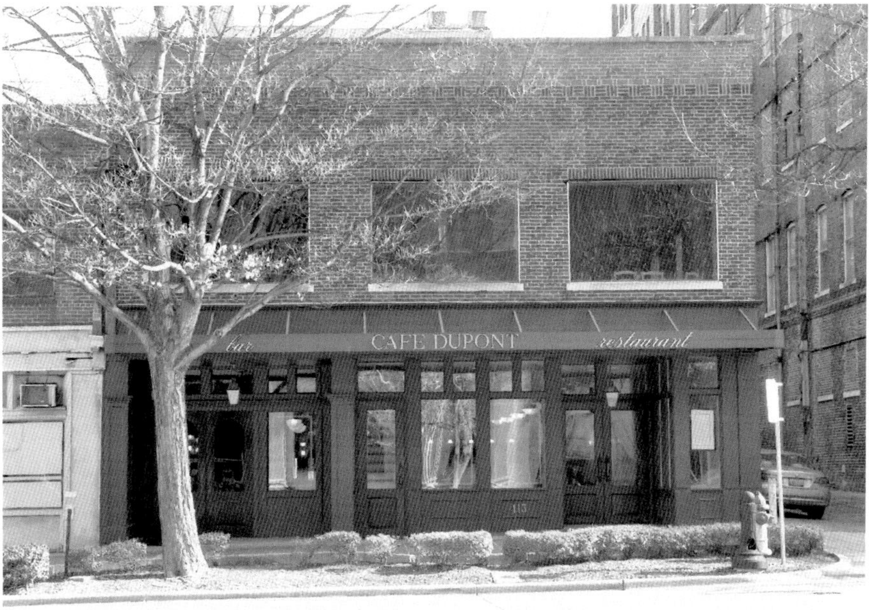

Outside Café Dupont in 2015. *Photograph by Emily Brown.*

College and graduating, Chef Dupont went back to the restaurant industry, moving between jobs in Birmingham and New Orleans in fine dining, working his way up the restaurant chain and even putting some time in at Frank Stitt's restaurants.

After nearly twenty years in the business, Chef Dupont decided he was ready to open his own restaurant and work for himself, but he had to choose between New Orleans and Birmingham as the place to make his mark. Chef Dupont knew he wanted to experiment more with fine cuisine than the typical customers in New Orleans would allow at the time—people came to New Orleans for Cajun food, not the nouvelle southern cuisine that has since spread across the Southeast. Birmingham seemed like the better choice for Chef Dupont since it would allow him room for more creativity.

"I knew as a chef I wanted to do more. I wanted to be fresh," Chef Dupont said. So he and his wife started looking around downtown Birmingham for a spot. His heart has always been in old buildings—from his time in New Orleans working in historic buildings and renovated churches, resplendent with stained glass and architectural details—but without a lot of money as a young chef, Chef Dupont had a hard time finding the right place for the right price. A chance trip antiquing in Springville, a small town just north and east of Birmingham, led Chef Dupont to a large historic space he could rent for just $350 a month, so he decided to open his restaurant there in 1994, far away from any ready-made crowds. "There are a lot of ups and downs of this culinary world of making your way," Chef Dupont said. "My food didn't match the area, and I was doing ten to fifteen people a night. That was a busy night. I'd do maybe twenty people for lunch. I realized within six months or so that this was not going well." But a Birmingham reporter had heard about the food Chef Dupont was creating in this renovated space and made the trip out to eat and write a review. She called Chef Dupont to tell him the review would be out in the Friday paper, and he hadn't even known she'd been in. "That reinvigorated my spirit, that somebody cares," Chef Dupont said. "That story came out that Friday and was a very lovely story. They loved it. The phone rang off the hook, and that was the beginning of managing some success." For the next seven years, Chef Dupont grew his business and served crowds more than willing to make the drive to Springville for a taste of his cuisine, allowing him to eventually buy his building there, but his dream of having a restaurant in downtown Birmingham continued. "That's my heart," he said.

By 2001, Chef Dupont was ready to start searching in downtown Birmingham again, and he found a building on Twentieth Street he could dismantle and rebuild into the high-end restaurant he'd dreamed of. Chef Dupont is well acquainted with the ups and downs of the restaurant business and knows some of the best lessons come from failures, but he said it took him a while to realize the level of risk he was taking moving into downtown at that time. "They had just taken off the whole front of the building. It was just an empty shell with no doors. I was sitting on a bucket of sheetrock thinking, 'What am I doing?' and I realize there's this parade of cars leaving Twentieth Street North. No one's even looking this way. I've invested everything I have into this moment, and no one's even looking. No one cares. Everyone's leaving this downtown area at five o'clock. That factor never did crystallize into my brain about where I was and what I was about to do, because I just thought if I could do it in Springville, I could surely do it in Birmingham." At first, people came because of the novelty of eating downtown, but they kept returning because of the quality of the food. Chef Dupont said it took almost four years to really change diners' traffic patterns and reestablish himself with a foothold in success. "I was there, holding the street open, every night. It was just myself," Chef Dupont said. "It wasn't on people's minds that downtown was a viable area for entertainment."

Chef Dupont's philosophy has always been to reinvest in his own business and, thereby, the economy of the city, which is why he bought and renovated both of the buildings that housed his restaurants and why, when he was ready for a new challenge, he did the same with the old site of a Kathy G. restaurant on Fourth Avenue and Nineteenth Street in 2011. The concept for his new restaurant, Mix Bakery, grew out of Chef Dupont's love of and admiration for Corey Hinkel's breads and pastries. Just a short walk from Café Dupont, Mix had different challenges drawing crowds from the nearby offices and banking buildings since the former restaurant had been closed for many years. "It was a great place," Chef Dupont said. "And it was funny how five blocks away from Café Dupont, the energy is totally different. We would do one hundred people every day for lunch." For three years, Chef Dupont poured his creative energy into Mix, and people responded well. But with a new concept for a casual lunch spot next door to Café Dupont in the works, Chef Dupont needed to make some changes. "I didn't want it to just go away, but I realized for it to go to the next level, it needed to be open at night and for brunch, and I wasn't interested in that," Chef Dupont said. "I found a way to not lose the business downtown, but to promote it and gain it, by including Carole [Griffin] in it." He brought Carole in for several weeks to get her acquainted with the space, and then she bought it from him to open Continental Bakery Downtown.

The latest venture for Chef Dupont promotes the customers' own creativity in making their meals. At Tau Poco, diners choose one selection from each section of the menu—protein, bread, side and two sauces—for a street-food-style lunch with flavors inspired by world cuisine. Meats like Korean pork or American-made sausage can be nestled in flatbreads or steam buns and topped with chimichurri or Sriracha aioli with a side of fried plantains or Israeli couscous for twelve thousand different combinations. Tau Poco is right next door to Café Dupont, a tiny space Chef Dupont renovated and opened for just $15,000, which got him and the restaurant written up in *Forbes* magazine. Chef Dupont said that Tau Poco represents that "entrepreneurial spirit" to him. "Ultimately as chefs and restaurant owners, we are all graded on food." No matter what the exterior or interior furnishings are of a restaurant, if the flavor and quality of the meal isn't up to par, customers won't return. "The show can only accent the quality you're putting on the plate," Chef Dupont said. He believes that putting his heart and soul and creative energy into the food he creates is what has kept his customers coming back, both in

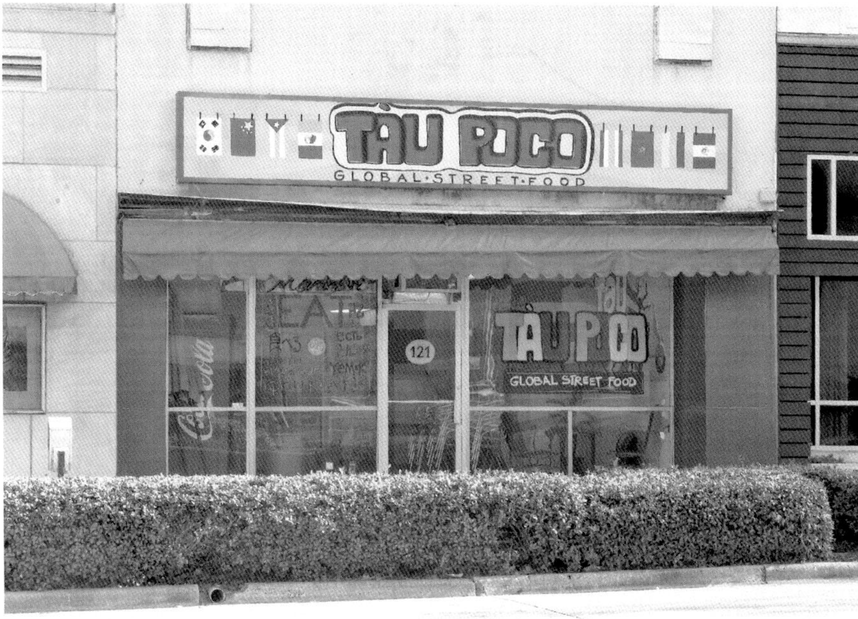

Outside Tau Poco in 2015. *Photograph by Emily Brown.*

Springville and now in downtown Birmingham, for over twenty years. "You can taste the difference," Chef Dupont said. "It boils down to the person cooking your food, that they really care about what you're tasting. It's one of those variables that you can't measure."

Chris Hastings and Hot and Hot Fish Club

Undoubtedly one of the most successful former members of Frank Stitt's team, Chef Chris Hastings and his Hot and Hot Fish Club in Southside have taken their place among the city's, and the country's, noteworthy chefs and restaurants in their own right. Since the restaurant opened in 1995, Chef Hastings and his wife and partner, Idie, have focused on providing the highest-quality local and seasonal ingredients prepared in their signature southern style. And while locals have long been acquainted with the special, welcoming and delicious experience that an evening at Hot and Hot entails, 2012 brought national attention to Chef Hastings when he bested Chef Bobby Flay on Food Network's *Iron Chef America*. More importantly, in 2012,

Chef Hastings won the sought-after James Beard Award Best Chef in the South, an award for which he'd been nominated twice before.

Before opening Hot and Hot Fish Club, Chef Hastings worked for Chef Stitt on two separate occasions: from 1986 to 1989, when he helped open Bottega as its head chef, and from 1991 to 1993, after returning from a stint in California, where he connected more fully to the farm-to-table movement. On opening Bottega, Chef Hastings said it was a great experience: "[It's] fantastic to go through an opening…and to really focus on Italian cuisine." But it was his experience in California—opening the Lark Creek Inn, where he bought everything the restaurant cooked from local farmers—that took all he had learned with Chef Stitt to the next level. Despite the influence and efforts of Chef Stitt to source from local purveyors in Birmingham, when Chef Hastings opened his restaurant in 1995, finding everything a chef would need to have a 100 percent farm-to-table restaurant was still difficult. The Hastings put the word out that they were looking for local food growers, even people with small, home gardens, to bring in organic produce for the restaurant's menus. "All the great fish out of the Gulf was there and a handful of farmers," Chef Hastings said. "But finding foragers, finding a whole array of different animals, was hard." Chef Hastings credits the start of the Pepper Place Farmers' Market with boosting the city's access to and knowledge about the wide variety of local foods we have available now. He said Pepper Place has been a huge influence providing access for regular people to local "produce and fruits, grains, beef, pork, chicken, cheeses, apiaries, all the things that only Frank and I and a handful of others had a long time ago." And the fact that these ingredients are all available at a local farmers market "is really important in terms of this community's access to a healthier food supply."

A visit to Hot and Hot Fish Club today showcases the impressive variety of sources Chef Hastings has developed over the years. Dishes like the famed Hot and Hot Tomato Salad, which comes with a pretty variety of heirloom tomatoes, field peas, corn, whole fried okra and topped with bacon are highly anticipated each year as the season for the ingredients approaches. Other favorite entrées include anything with pork from Fudge Family Farms or fresh Gulf shrimp or fish. Even the plates at Hot and Hot come from a local source. Potter Tena Payne of Earthborn Pottery handcrafts all the plates, salt dishes, serving pieces and more for the entire restaurant, a touch that lends a warmth to the already welcoming atmosphere. Hot and Hot is famed for its open kitchen, and interested diners can choose to sit at the Chef's Table, really the long bar flanking the kitchen and prep area, to watch as chefs plate sizzling appetizers or chop garnishes for desserts like the Hot and Hot Doughnuts or Chocolate Soufflé. The restaurant's wine list has earned the Hastings accolades, but its cocktail list has revolutionized the craft cocktail scene in Birmingham with its "Farm to Glass" concept, using southern spirits in a lot of cases and local and foraged ingredients for syrups and more. Idie Hastings manages the front of the house and bookkeeping, and Chef Hastings admits that part of the business is what sets good restaurants apart, aside from their food. "We're in the hospitality business," he said. "We're here to make people happy through food and service. Hospitality in that true southern way is really one of our great strengths to our business. Our restaurant conveys that warmth and hospitality and energy…partly from the open kitchen, that feels good…That's our philosophy as a business. We want the place to feel good and everybody to feel welcome."

Like any chef with long-term success and sustainability, Chef Hastings has learned that his ability to grow and change keeps him hitting the mark with customers who are becoming more educated about their food. "Interest in food is an important piece to their quality of life," Chef Hastings said. "People are really dialed in to food and know more about techniques and ingredients." So over the past twenty years he's had to evolve to keep up, growing from a simple restaurant focused on seasonal ingredients to a more technically driven style of cooking focused on craftsmanship. He mentions their charcuterie program in particular as part of this growth, using whole animals and expanding what they have to offer. The restaurant "has more of a modernist approach, precise, clean, detailed in its composition and flavor profiles," Chef Hastings said. "For our guests, I think they appreciate our evolution…Restaurants that never changed their menus and they stay within the context of where they were when they opened and they don't grow and change with times, to me that's very risky." Birmingham's evolving dining culture plays a role in keeping Chef Hastings on his toes as well. "There's a lot of competition out there," he says, "a lot of good cooks doing different things, and that keeps the restaurant here very healthy…To survive you have to know exactly who you are, you have to compete for customers. If everybody has to grow and react, that winner is the customer."

Seeking this success through competition has kept Chef Hastings inspired over the years, as has the desire to keep his business dynamic for the next twenty years, but he said the heart of his creative inspiration always boils down to the food. "What inspires me always is and always will be the ingredients and the farmers and the people who actually bring us these amazing ingredients," he said. "Those ingredients, really as a creative person and a chef, are the things that keep our creative juices flowing and at the top of our game. We have to respect and articulate our vision through the ingredients without stepping on them or overdoing it. That's where the magic is in great cooking." The authenticity of the food at Hot and Hot is evidence that Chef Hastings spends a lot of time visiting farmers' markets around the state, putting on cooking demonstrations and meeting with farmers and patrons alike to stay connected to those ingredients and those sources.

Chef Hastings has become not only a major player in the local and regional food scene through his own restaurant but also through his work consulting with other restaurants, bringing his philosophy of locally rooted cuisine that tells the story of a place to other establishments seeking revitalization or help in starting up. From his work with Standard Bistro in Mount Laurel and Springhouse on Lake Martin with its James Beard–nominated chef Rob McDaniel to consulting with artisan popsicle food truck 80 Pops, Chef Hastings reinforces his belief that sourcing locally and seasonally will encourage success in any restaurant venture. "Food is unique in that you can source from that place and tell the story of that place, and any place you go it's different," he said. He's even been planning a second restaurant for himself, a more casual restaurant in Charlie Thigpen's Garden Gallery at Pepper Place, to be called Ovenbird. This small restaurant in the garden and small interior space will feature only food cooked over wood. No gas lines will be installed in the facility. "If we want to boil water, we'll have to build a fire," Chef Hastings said. "So that will be exciting." Far from just the smoked meats traditional to the South that wood cooking brings to mind, the idea for Ovenbird is to marry other wood cooking cultures, like those of Argentina or Portugal or Spain, with Chef Hastings's southern roots. Customers can expect to see cooking over ash, cooking in coals in cast iron, smoking large hams in the stove's flue and other creative techniques for the food at Ovenbird.

Winning the James Beard Award in 2012 brought national attention to Chef Hastings and to Birmingham, and he said that aside from maintaining a successful restaurant for twenty years, that award is his proudest accomplishment, something he and his wife worked for every day since they served their first dish at Hot and Hot Fish Club. Winning *Iron Chef* against Bobby Flay, where the Hot and Hot team were the first contestants ever to bring their own whole set of dishes and maybe even the first to bring moonshine, also garnered a lot of attention, but Chef Hastings said that experience was a win for him just in being asked to participate and showcase what true, modern southern cuisine is like. The accolades even brought Travel

Channel's Andrew Zimmern and his *Bizarre Foods America* to Birmingham, where he visited with Chef Hastings and two of his former employees at their food truck, Shindigs, which features local, seasonal ingredients as well.

Chef Hastings sees this new generation of chefs in Birmingham—including his mentees and their roles in the burgeoning food truck scene and chefs at places like Post Office Pies, El Barrio and Brick and Tin—as a sign of Birmingham's evolution as a foodie town. He remembers Birmingham of the 1970s and 1980s as a place "kind of locked in time, not really evolving like the rest of the country," where Alice Waters and sustainable sourcing were gaining popularity. "Then Frank showed up, and we gravitated more toward this evolution of food in America," Chef Hastings said. The next wave of restaurants included his own and made more chefs and customers care a great deal about the quality and source of their ingredients. "Now you've got a ton of really great restaurants," Chef Hastings said. "And a large majority are graduates from mine or Frank's kitchen…All of that is a really cool sign that the evolution is continuing. You're seeing not only new restaurants but a diversity of restaurants, a food truck scene that's providing both entrepreneurs access to getting a business started and the customer access to delicious affordable food." From casual to fine dining, Birmingham's current food culture really is a credit to the dedication of chefs like Chris Hastings, who forged the way for better sourcing and insisted on quality above all else.

James Lewis and Bettola

Though not of the Frank Stitt or Chris Hastings lineage, one Birmingham restaurateur made his own way into the national spotlight with a James Beard Award nomination and was at the forefront of the city's movement toward more casual restaurants that still offer the highest-quality ingredients and attention to detail we've come to expect from those higher-end establishments. James Lewis opened his first restaurant, Bettola, in 2006 with the idea to take the simplicity of ingredients in Italian cooking and combine them with his soulful approach to feeding people, but his Birmingham and cooking roots go back much further than that.

In the 1950s, Chef Lewis's grandfather ran several restaurants in Birmingham, including a coffee shop, a place called the Melba Café and a restaurant called Jefferson Seafood on First Avenue near the old Sears building. Chef Lewis said Jefferson Seafood was a place where doctors and lawyers would come to enjoy the oyster bar after work or on the weekends. A dedication to hard work kept Chef Lewis's grandfather busy earning a living, and his grandmother raised their children, including Chef Lewis's mother. That commitment and work ethic have inspired Chef Lewis in his own career, but he credits cooking with his grandmother with forging his relationship with food and the power it can have to create a satisfying experience, on all levels. "That connection really stuck with me throughout the years," Chef Lewis said. "So when I look at food or when I'm in that zone of cooking, I've tried to put that kind of love and energy into what I'm doing so it comes out honestly. It's not just about making money. It's just my passion of what I love to do."

Born in Montreal, James Lewis and his family returned to Birmingham and his mother's family when he was four years old. They spent several years here, but then they moved to California when Chef Lewis was nine at the start of the movement toward healthy eating in the 1970s. Being surrounded by a care for quality ingredients at an early age gave Chef Lewis a desire to educate himself more about food, and he began his restaurant career at the age of fifteen, first bussing tables at a pancake restaurant and then working in the front of the house as a wait assistant. Throughout high school and college, Chef Lewis worked his way up to fine dining, both in the kitchen and out front, in an upscale Italian restaurant first and then in a Michelin-starred restaurant called the Plumed Horse, which is still in operation. In his early twenties, Chef Lewis found his way back to Birmingham and several restaurant kitchens here, but it was really his annual trips to Italy that gave him the idea to open his own Italian-style restaurant. "I was more intrigued with how they can make simple food so amazing," Chef Lewis said. "So it just got me thinking back into the ingredients and into food, where it comes from and how it's utilized."

Since it opened, Bettola has made a unique mark on Birmingham's dining scene both because the quality of the food at a more accessible price point was a new idea to the city and because Chef Lewis's approach to Italian food is fresh and satisfying without succumbing to the heavy plates of pasta most Italian joints are known for. Of course Bettola does pasta—and it does it well—but the purity of the sauces and locally sourced vegetables that accompany it keep the food vibrant. Pizza from the wood-fire oven is authentically Tuscan, with minimal toppings and cheese so the combination of flavors has a chance to shine. The antipasti platters and salads remain customer favorites as well. And of course, utilizing the freshest produce from local farmers, just like high-end restaurants around town, has always been key. "I love dealing with those local farmers," Chef Lewis said. "I've got a handful of guys that I really deal with, and it's so great to get that purity picked out of the ground. I want to get that transferred onto the plate. They're growing different things, and I try and formulate what I'm doing around that."

In 2012, Chef Lewis expanded his restaurant aspirations into the space next door to Bettola with a casual restaurant—named Vittoria after the Italian spelling of his grandmother's name—focused on unique cuts of meat and small plates. With Vittoria, the same emphasis was placed on purity and authenticity, but customers were offered things like lamb or duck in addition to pork, beef and poultry, plus local produce and an expanded list of craft cocktails. Chef Lewis said the next step for both restaurants was a move toward combining and harmonizing their efforts. The evolution revamped Bettola's space and menu; created more connection between the two restaurants, both physically and philosophically; and dropped the Vittoria name for the blended concept. "I really want to showcase a lot of different ingredients," Chef Lewis said, to give customers a different perspective while maintaining "a really close focus on freshness and just merging of flavors and honesty, honesty of flavors. What makes me the happiest is to give to others. That's the most primal thing that I know. I want to get back to that and make that experience pleasurable for people."

Birmingham was ready for restaurants like Bettola and Vittoria in no small part because the city has been educated about quality food by pioneers like Frank Stitt and Chris Hastings. "I wonder how this food city would be without [Frank] even being involved here," Chef Lewis said. "Would it have been a lot later on that it would have happened? He stays honest to what he does and what he wants to give to the community. I think that's been a great foundation for a lot of other people in the food industry and the standard that everyone needs to be on the playing field. I love the community sense of how people work together and trade and barter…helping each other out. It's great."

Taking the lessons of those chefs and the education they'd started in diners allowed chefs like Chef Lewis and others around town to open this style of fast casual restaurant committed to quality ingredients. "When we started doing that, the idea was using the same quality ingredients as an upper-end restaurant but in a casual environment so you can come back and dress the way you want to dress and…it was all about the food," Chef Lewis said. He wants to make his customers "feel welcome in a place that they can connect with on a weekly basis." Chef Lewis also credits the incredible work of Pepper Place Farmers' Market with providing access to better ingredients and educating the city's residents about quality food. "It's very powerful right now. It's one of the top markets in the country," Chef Lewis said. "People love it and connect with it. If we didn't have that, what would that be like right now? Each key component in the city, what would it be like if that didn't happen? Demanding and having that kind of quality is better for your body, it's better for your lifestyle."

Clif and Maureen Holt and Little Savannah

When Chef Clif Holt of Little Savannah in Forest Park began his culinary career, and even while working under Frank Stitt at Highlands Bar and Grill, he took for granted the practice of sourcing fresh produce locally. Since he'd come from a background in engineering and architectural design before deciding to open his restaurant with his wife, Maureen, in 2003, he just thought local sourcing was what everyone did. But once he began having to buy vegetables for his own restaurant, he realized with surprise that a lot of farmers worked essentially as brokers for produce from far away. Growing up in Cullman, like Frank Stitt, Chef Clif Holt had a lot of exposure to Alabama's lush farmland, and with a grandmother whose cooking taught him the advantages of fresh and seasonal vegetables, he knew there had to be a better way. When Pepper Place Farmers' Market was first getting started, about the same time Little Savannah was, Chef Clif attended a meeting for farmers and chefs who wanted to be involved, and he sensed a real turnaround happening in Birmingham, mostly through the influence of chefs like Frank Stitt and Chris Hastings demanding better-quality ingredients. Farmers who attended the Pepper Place meeting and said they intended to broker tomatoes and lettuce and other vegetables not their own or from nearby farms were politely invited by market organizers to take their business elsewhere. Pepper Place organizers had clear intentions to focus only on the produce and products that Alabama has to offer. "It's not like the farm-to-table movement is anything new," Chef Clif said. "It's in a revitalization state, a renewal state."

The second key to the Holts' becoming the passionate advocates for local farms and fresh, seasonal eating that they are today came when Chef Clif got sick from eating a pre-cut, commercially raised steak purchased at a mega chain. Research into big-business food systems led him to the realization that his steak had been treated with formaldehyde, a substance many people are allergic to, and he committed himself to the idea of food being more than just something to satisfy our hunger—it can also be a major source of health and nutrition. More research sent Chef Clif to Auburn University with two samples of fennel, one raised commercially and one grown at a local farm with sustainable practices like crop rotation and soil nutrition. Not only did the two samples taste distinctly different, but they also broke down into very different elements. The commercial fennel was essentially water and cells while the organic and local fennel contained actual nutritional content. This confirmation of Chef Clif's beliefs about sustainable farming was a life changer. "That really is kind of the basis from where our view stems," he said. "Our health and welfare is based on what we consume, and also the health and welfare of our farmers. If a farmer is driving a Cadillac, something is going right in the system. My desire is to support them as much as possible. When you demand different, you're going to get different down the road. That can change our health and quality of life."

So since 2003, Chef Clif has been crafting menus that change with each season and are based on the best produce available. During the summer, when more is grown and harvested, Chef Clif sources from fifteen to eighteen farmers for dishes like a watermelon salad with mint. When produce selection is leaner in the cooler months, Chef Clif still focuses on the best of what's in season in Alabama. The Holts even have a small garden at the back of their funky, artsy space that produces herbs like thyme, rosemary, lemon balm, mint, parsley, sage, dill, chives, lavender and garlic for their food and their eclectic cocktail menu. They bottle and sell the mix for their signature spicy peach margarita, but other cocktails change with the season, just like the food, which is southern inspired but always surprising in its fresh approach. Though an occasional source of a few tomatoes, peas and the like, the garden's function, Chef Clif says, is mostly so they can "stay within the understanding of it all" because he knows it's not possible to be both a farmer and a cook. "I found that finding good products, produce, meats, components you can work with makes a big difference," Chef Clif says. "Letting them speak for themselves, staying within the season, helps us stay within a focus of what we're trying to do. It keeps it more concise."

This focus and attention to detail that shines through the food can also be admired in the atmosphere at Little Savannah. Bartenders stock the shelves with unique varieties of spirits, syrups and mixers and are always ready to craft a special drink to suit any taste. From the art on the walls to the intimate and rustic tables, or even a seat in the patio garden, diners at Little Savannah feel invited and welcome into the very personal space. But perhaps the highlight of the dining experience, if there can be one other than the food, is to sit and watch the neighborhood foot traffic out the windows, which only adds to the vibrancy of the evening's meal.

Though Chef Clif Holt knows the pathways broken before him have made sourcing locally somewhat easier, finding quality ingredients available in the quantities he needs can still be a challenge. In order to get a wider variety of fruits, not just vegetables, that he's interested in working with, Chef Clif has even been known to purchase seeds of the exact varieties he wants for farmers to grow. Developing those types of give-and-take, back-and-forth relationships benefits everyone, from farmer to chef and restaurant patron. Another way the Holts strive to support farmers is by hosting weekly Community Farm Table dinners at Little Savannah. The dinners, inspired by the idea of strengthening relationships between the people who grow food and the people who buy food, are family style and served at one table that seats farmers with regular diners. These Community Farm Tables also generally benefit a local cause, as well. Growing exposure to these dinners has become a priority for the Holts, both to deepen their customers' relationships with their farmers and to spotlight what beautiful food they're growing on those farms.

After a decade of running the restaurant, Maureen Holt decided to follow through on one of her lifelong dreams: attending culinary school. It was something she'd been thinking about since she started in the restaurant business at fifteen and during her early days working at Bottega and cooking with good friends in her time off. As one of nine children, Chef Maureen Holt also grew up in an atmosphere full of cooking, where every sibling had kitchen responsibilities, from making meatballs to helping with dishes for big family Thanksgivings. In deciding what the future for Little Savannah should hold, Chef Maureen decided to attend the San Francisco Cooking School, a sixteen-week intensive in training followed by an eight-week externship in a restaurant kitchen. Chef Maureen shared how fun and educational it was to go incognito as a restaurant owner during this time, where the focus was on learning techniques and practicing skills for the kitchen rather than the front-of-house business in which she'd flourished. She took their daughter with her to California and, every day, walked her to a school that taught Mandarin, and they both soaked up the atmosphere of San Francisco's deeply embedded farm-to-table culture on Chef Maureen's weekends off from school—a rare luxury for a restaurateur. "I feel like there's a better understanding and a better rapport with the kitchen staff," Chef Maureen says of her expanded role at Little Savannah. "Being a woman and being a restaurateur is a little different as well. It feels good to have gone through that program and feel confident."

Chef Maureen has long shared her husband's passion for supporting local farmers and showcasing the best in local ingredients. Her time spent in San Francisco has allowed her to bring her new love of making pastas and pastries to the Little Savannah menu with dishes like a Cullman County Sweet Potato Puree with Ravioli or Churros and Olive Oil cake added to the dessert menu, which she recently revamped, dishes that maintain the restaurant's southern roots while branching into other cultural flavor influences. "There's lots of other cooking methods I'm aware of now," Chef Maureen said. And Chef Maureen doesn't just believe in local ingredients for their quality and taste; she's also been a past member of Birmingham's Food Policy Council, a group working to find ways to improve the city and state's food systems. Through her work with the Food Policy Council, Chef Maureen spent time with Taylor Clark during the budding stages of the Urban Food Project, having talks and brainstorming sessions together about ways to expand the market for farmers outside the scope of Pepper Place Farmers' Market and eventually becoming one of the first regular customers of the Urban Food Project. Little Savannah has even hosted a few Community Farm Table dinners to benefit the Urban Food Project. "I think it's a viable product," Chef Maureen said.

With her new skills and responsibilities at Little Savannah, Chef Maureen plans to expand Little Savannah's presence with more cooking classes, another passion of hers. Little Savannah already holds two monthly cooking classes, for which Chefs Clif and Maureen alternate responsibilities, and she hopes to offer more consistent classes as well as potentially take their lessons on the road, perhaps somewhere like Chef Clif Holt's hometown, Cullman, which has grown a lot in recent years as well. The restaurant itself is always in a state of growth, with recent changes to the flow of entering and seating serving to modernize the space and better accommodate customers for an enjoyable dining experience. With the restaurant growth also in nearby Avondale—with restaurants like Melt, Post Office Pies and more opening since 2013—Chef Maureen hopes for a stronger connection between the two neighborhoods, creating pathways to make the city more walkable since so many great dining options are opening up. "What's nice now is hopefully we're finding more people that are cooking fresh and buying more local products on a day-to-day basis," Chef Maureen said. "As we continue in the Birmingham restaurant industry, you're going to see more and more of that.

It should be just a given. We've been talking about it for ten years. Hopefully, people are demanding it now, that the arugula on their burger or salad came from one of our Alabama farmers at least."

Though Chef Clif is pleased to watch the growth Birmingham's farm-to-table movement has seen since he opened Little Savannah, he knows there's still more that can be done to encourage a healthy food system:

> *I give Frank Stitt and Chris Hastings both multiple thumbs up in affecting us to the point where we're aware of* [the farm-to-table movement], *and we're in a position to carry on the tradition and direction. I feel like the momentum is there, but the relationship between farmer and chef needs to be stronger on both parts. I think we need more farms, more chefs, more people interested in the creativity of cooking. I feel like there's a huge opportunity for the upcoming generations to turn farming into a lucrative…not just monetarily lucrative…but a lucrative lifestyle.*

Birmingham is lucky to have two people this passionate about the health of our food system and the health that it can pass on to our citizens.

George Reis and Ocean

Proving that Birmingham is still a seafood restaurant town at heart, one restaurateur in town has made providing creative dishes from the best of Alabama seafood in not just one but two local restaurants his mission. George Reis opened Ocean just up from Five Points South in 2002 and has been serving eager crowds of fine diners fresh seafood and other local specialties ever since. Though not originally from Birmingham, Chef Reis still came into the restaurant business through a strong family influence. "My parents have always been crazy about food," he said. "It was always a big thing at our house." He started out washing dishes and busing tables in his native New York, working his way up through the restaurant ranks, and then traveled and worked in restaurants around the country, eventually finding his way to the Gulf Coast. Being surrounded by the bounty of the ocean, the freshest seafood possible, Chef Reis became inspired. So when the chance came to open his own place in Birmingham, which is lucky to be positioned close enough to the Gulf for easy access to fresh seafood, he took the plunge. "I felt there was room in town for someone to focus on seafood," Chef Reis said. "I did a lot of seafood, and it was a natural extension."

Having a fine-dining option for really good seafood made Ocean and Chef Reis a success, so when the space next door to Ocean became available in 2006, he decided to expand into it and open a spot with a more casual atmosphere. Ocean's more relaxed sister, 26 still offered the best ingredients from Birmingham and the Gulf, but it also allowed Chef Reis to get creative in new ways without having to run all over town to a new restaurant. "Why worry about being somewhere else?" Chef Reis said, though he admits having dedicated, hardworking and creative staff also makes his job easier. "I give a lot of autonomy to the two sous chefs who work for me. As they come up with creative ideas, I try to make sure they stay apart. We purposely keep the price points different. You're challenged to find great products and good stuff." That search for creativity led Chef Reis to change up 26 in early 2015, reworking the casual eatery into an oyster bar also focused on serving craft beer and cocktails.

Sourcing local ingredients has been part of Chef Reis's business model since the mid-1990s and his time in the Gulf. Fishermen would bring in seafood daily, fresh off their boats, but local farms in South Alabama also provided produce and artisan cheeses. "I always felt it was a great thing to do," Chef Reis said. "It's fun and neat to see what's around you." Now at both restaurants, Chef Reis makes a point to find out not only exactly where his fish come from but also who the fishermen are who provide it and what kind of businesses they operate to make sure the quality of his ingredients is always the best. "Without being oceanfront, we need to go and find out who is catching our fish in the Gulf," he said. "We work really closely to make sure we know who they are in the boat." Depending on the season, you can find oysters, raw and cooked, in a variety of sauces; fish like red snapper served over a bed of cheese grits with ham and sautéed vegetables; and even sushi on Ocean's menu. Ocean is still the more romantic choice, with wood accents and private tables or booths while the new restaurant is a great place to unwind with co-workers and friends.

Aside from operating two bustling restaurants, Chef Reis has made a name for himself in town by being instrumental in founding Birmingham Originals, a national group with local chapters dedicated to celebrating and supporting independent restaurants. "A group of chefs got together and wanted to find ways to keep people focused on what's happening in the community," Chef Reis said. The group covers the gamut of restaurants, from the high end, such as his Ocean, to the more casual and even small cafés. All manner of independent kitchens are celebrated by Birmingham Originals. "We're people in your community," Chef Reis said. "I live here. My boys go to school here. I employee people who live here. We're taking the idea of local produce and famers and saying, 'Hey, these are home-grown restaurants,' we need the same mentality of support."

From the kitchen and waitstaff to a focus on providing great meals and dining experiences to the customers, the values of support and celebrating what's local flow through both of Chef Reis's restaurants. "Everybody really is on the same page," he said. "Our goal is to take care of guests who come through the door. It's not rocket science. It's just really good food served really well." And though hospitality as a southern grace might not have been encoded into Chef Reis from birth, he's certainly adopted the ideals of service in his career. "We're doing well and happy with the guests who we get, happy with repeat clientele who we love. We're going along loving life."

Chris Newsome and Ollie Irene

Another former Frank Stitt employee, Chris Newsome, with his wife, Anna, opened a small gastropub in the Over-the-Mountain Community of Mountain Brook in 2011. Named for Chris's paternal grandmother, Ollie Irene has gained a loyal following of neighborhood and area residents alike for its thoughtfully crafted food that celebrates seasonal ingredients. Chris runs the kitchen and Anna runs the front of the house, and she said the choice to use local and seasonal ingredients wasn't as much a choice as a natural extension of the way the best chefs have always worked. "The best flavors and quality come from honest products that are in season and nearby, grown with great care, integrity and attention," she said. "We source ingredients this way because we treat them this way in the kitchen."

Menu items like mussels, an English-style pub breakfast, catfish and fresh pasta constantly evolve and come paired with produce and more from local farms such as Mount Laurel Farm, Stone Hollow Farmstead, Terra Preta and J3 Organics. In the restaurant's beginnings, some of its regulars were even inspired to bring in the bounty from their home gardens for the chefs to cook up, meaning one customer's turnip greens or honey might have come from her neighbor's yard. As a pub, Ollie Irene is also known for specialty cocktails created with house-made syrups, local draft beer and a quality wine list. Its desserts, such as the Sweet Potato Turnover topped with a homemade marshmallow, are seasonal, too.

With a nomination from the James Beard Foundation in 2012 as Best New Restaurant, Ollie Irene has become a favorite of many locals for great food in a warm, inviting atmosphere, much like the legendary kitchen of Chef Newsome's grandmother did. "Naming the restaurant Ollie Irene is a way to honor that memory of simple, open-armed hospitality and homegrown food, and the associated farming heritage in the South," said Anna. "At Ollie Irene, Chef Newsome is not re-creating his grandmother's food but rather continuing a tradition of cooking using fresh and seasonal ingredients and hosting all who stop in at mealtime."

7
FARM SOURCING

With all the quality restaurants in Birmingham serving local ingredients at almost any price point, it's easy to forget that sourcing local eggs, grass-fed beef, stone-ground grits, peak-season tomatoes and corn, Gulf seafood and more hasn't always been so easy. Fertile Alabama land, bordered on one end by the coast, and our long growing season provide the perfect atmosphere for this locavore culture, but people in Birmingham still had to warm up to the idea of seasonal, rather than convenience, eating. Demand from local chefs who have committed to serving local ingredients and supporting local farmers and purveyors, plus a willingness from these small businesspeople to try something new—try growing organic, try planting heirloom seeds, try partnering with chefs—slowly built up enough momentum to be called a local food movement. Nowhere is this movement more evident than at the multiple farmers' markets found across the city. Any day of the week, Birmingham residents can find an open farmers' market selling goods raised in Alabama soil, and at some of the busier markets, shoppers might see a cooking demo from one local chef while watching another pick out greens for that night's menu. These markets, and the farmers who fill them, are a significant part of Birmingham's food and restaurant landscape, so they deserve attention for how they've filled our plates with the freshest seasonal ingredients both at home and in dining rooms across the city.

Finley Avenue Farmers' Market

Founded in 1921 by the Jefferson County Truck Growers Association, what's now known as the Finley Avenue Farmers' Market remains one of the oldest farmers markets in the country. In the 1920s, finding a steady market for their produce was difficult for farmers, so a group of them, mostly Italian immigrants, decided to band together to create a permanent space where they could sell their lettuce, tomatoes, squash and more. This small group of farmers wanted to form a co-op that would allow them to pool their resources and expand their buying power for supplies in bulk. Eventually, they settled on a site at First Avenue North, across from what would become Niki's Restaurant, and residents from across the city could come to buy fresh vegetables direct from the farmers.

In about 1956, the group decided to relocate to its current site on Finley Avenue just north of downtown. Easy access to the interstate keeps this location convenient for farmers and customers. Now, the Finley Avenue market is run by a board of nine plus a manager hired to run day-to-day

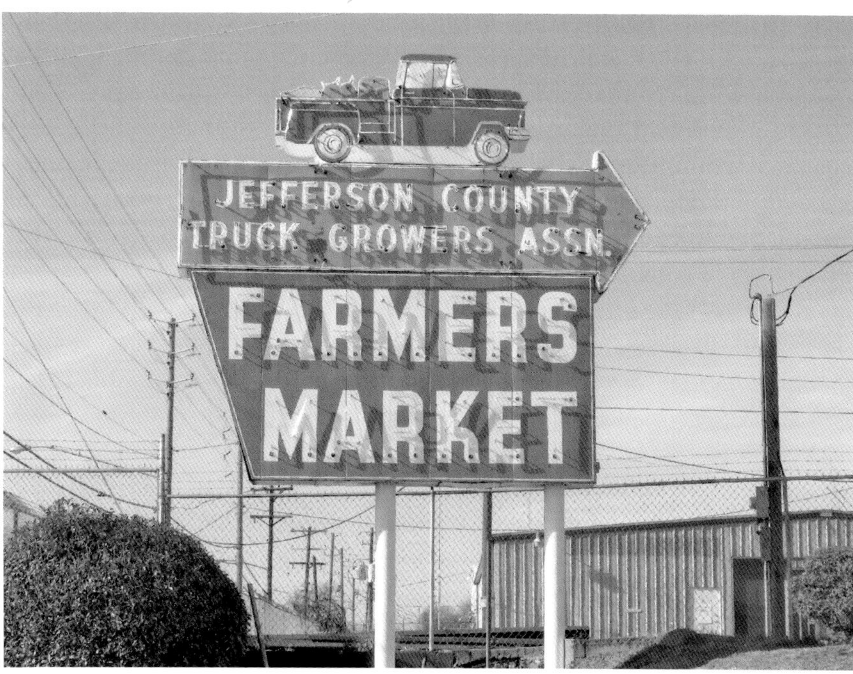

The sign outside Alabama Farmers' Market on Finley Avenue in 2015. *Photograph by Emily Brown.*

operations. The large lot is lined with roofed and open-sided sheds that farmers can rent by the day, month or year, plus a central area that contains a more formal market selling Alabama-made products like honey and jams in addition to the produce. A lot of the tenants at Finley Avenue are still local farmers, hauling in their goods from their farms outside of town, but some of the spaces are taken up with commercially farmed goods. The ratio between commercial and local just depends on the season. Unlike the Pepper Place Farmers' Market, which is known for its heirloom and unusual varieties, Finley Market remains committed to serving popular items like sweet potatoes and watermelon, and Finley Avenue is the perfect place to go to buy in bulk vegetables like tomatoes for canning.

Pepper Place Farmers' Market

One of the most influential farmers' markets in terms of building the farm-to-table movement in Birmingham, Pepper Place Farmers' Market bustles with energy each Saturday from April to December, attracting visitors from across the metro area and surrounding suburbs. On Market Saturdays, visitors can expect to find around one hundred tents shading farm vendors who are selling seasonal produce from green beans to eggplants, local bakers and pastry chefs offering delicious pies and breads, vendors with honey collected from backyard hives or artisan cheese from goats and sheep, makers of jellies and sauces and chutneys displaying their jars alongside artists showcasing crafts and yard art and paintings and live music and weekly cooking demonstrations from the city's best chefs. Since 2000, Pepper Place has grown and expanded as it has come to define local food culture in Birmingham.

Held in the large lot next to the site of the former Dr. Pepper Syrup Plant and in the street next to the Martin Biscuit Company building, Pepper Place began with the vision of Cathy Sloss Jones, president of Sloss Real Estate. After visiting other cities around the country and noticing how culture flourished in these places because of their bustling farmers' markets, Cathy felt Birmingham could use this influx of energy in the historic Lakeview District, where her family's real estate business had already invested in redevelopment.

Originally known as Lakeview Park and designed as an entertainment district for Birmingham in the 1890s, Lakeview was home to the artificial

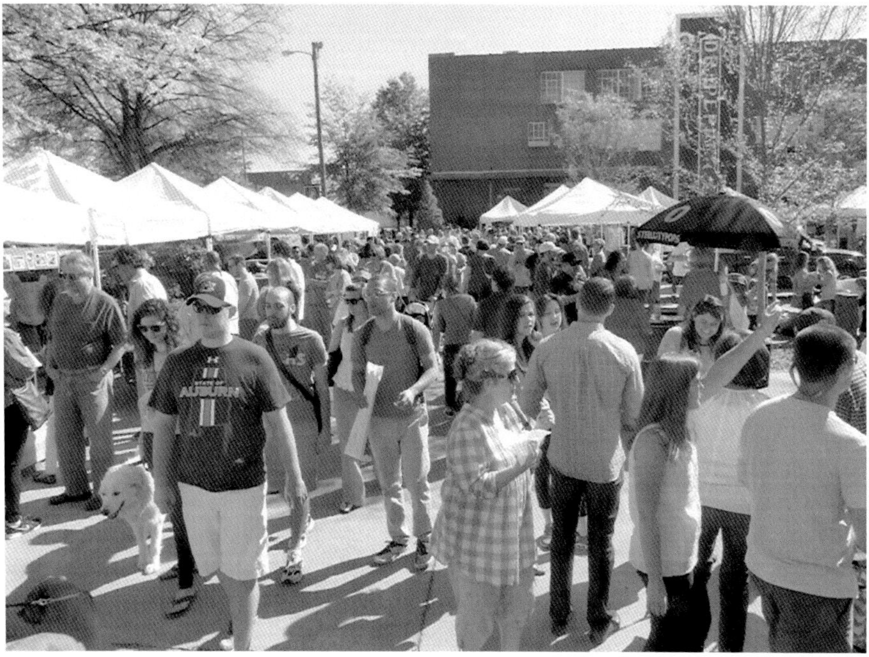

The crowd on a typical Saturday at Pepper Place Farmers' Market. *Photograph by James Brown.*

lake that gave the district its name as well as a swimming pool, a skating rink, a bowling alley and the ballpark that hosted the first Alabama-Auburn football game in 1893. During the Depression, the Birmingham Kiwanis Club helped secure the area's future by encouraging new businesses to build in the district, including the syrup plant and biscuit company whose painted logos still grace their buildings' structures. The original lake and amenities didn't survive the city's changes over time, and many of the businesses in the Lakeview District eventually closed; however, through the efforts of Sloss Real Estate, the area now called the Pepper Place Complex thrives and encompasses seven historic buildings that house a theater, several restaurants—including two from James Beard Award–winning chefs—a jazz club and a pilates studio and are home to the Pepper Place Farmers' Market each week.

The Sloss family could be the most influential members of Birmingham, as patriarch Colonel James Withers Sloss opened, in 1882, the large furnaces on First Avenue North that drew thousands to the city for work. Still an iconic part of Birmingham's skyline, Sloss Furnaces created vast numbers of jobs in the iron and steel industry that made the city what it was in the early days. Now, under the direction of Cathy Sloss Jones, the colonel's great-great-granddaughter, the company focuses on revitalization through redevelopment and construction.

With the combination of her family's dedication to Birmingham through business and development, her vision for the city's possibilities and ideas she gained while traveling around the country, Cathy was in the perfect position to begin Pepper Place Farmers' Market, though she was missing the key element: farmers to fill it. Such an enterprise required a lot of organization, so Cathy enlisted the help of Chef Frank Stitt of Highlands Bar and Grill and Chef Franklin Biggs of Homewood Gourmet, both of whom have served on the market's board, to help make connections to local farmers who might want to participate in such a market. One farmer in particular, Danny Jones of Durbin Farms in Clanton, introduced Cathy to many of the other farmers who participated in the early market, which was a far cry from the event that spans two blocks and hosts peak crowds nearing eight thousand currently.

Just a few farmers hauled in vegetables each week, selling their produce in a venue that must have been unfamiliar and strange: tents in a parking lot far from where the city's residents lived and dined at that time. Pepper Place was a little ahead of the national popularity of local farmers' markets, so Cathy was essentially creating a new way for citizens to shop and a new way for farmers to sell. Market manager Lisa Beasley, who came on board the project in 2009, shared that the beginnings of Pepper Place were a struggle for Cathy. At the time, finding fresh produce inside the city limits wasn't really possible, and building those relationships with farmers and getting them to try a new venue took some convincing. "She realized that a lot of our family farms were at risk in Alabama and felt like this would be a good opportunity to help them make more money and stay in business, and it has been," said Lisa. Over the years, the goals of the market have evolved from just providing access to fresh, local produce and revitalizing the area to connecting local chefs with farmers so they can more easily source ingredients for their menus, which is now one of the market's major functions. Lisa shared that bringing people from the farming and restaurant communities together on the market's board, providing a place for connections and conversations, has influenced the market's growth and success beyond measure. With deep roots in the Birmingham community keeping them committed to the market's continued prosperity, Lisa said both she and Cathy actively plan for Pepper Place's future beyond their own involvement. "Long after we're gone, we want to protect it," she said.

Aside from becoming a hub for community and offering healthy options for produce and more, Lisa believes one of the other important functions of Pepper Place is supporting the local economy. By helping small business owners, farmers and chefs alike, the market helps create a more stable and sustainable economy for the entire state and, by extension, the South. "That's rewarding and important," Lisa said. By fostering small, family-owned businesses for over a decade, cultivating relationships and helping young farmers begin and grow in their own successes, Pepper Place has remade the landscape for Birmingham restaurants. "I know that our relationships between farmers and local chefs have changed our local restaurant culture," she said. "It didn't happen overnight. It was a commitment by our farmers to try something different, and it was a lot of our local chefs who were willing to ask for what they wanted and what they'd like to have." Once the market organizers did their job of bringing the two groups together for these conversations, they could step back and watch the relationships blossom. "I know I can go to Little Savannah or Dyron's and find lettuce grown at Owl's Hollow or know the wood burning in the stove was delivered by Averiett Branch," Lisa said, something that wouldn't have been possible—or, at least, would have been much more difficult and only seen in smaller volume—before Pepper Place Farmers' Market began.

The future of Pepper Place as a part of Birmingham's cultural and foodie scene seems secure, though there's always room for growth. Though the market runs through the fall and into the beginning of December, crowds for the cooler months or on rainy days can be smaller, so a more permanent structure like a large covered pavilion where vendors could stay dry would be an ideal next step, something Lisa said they're working to build with the input of architects, city planners, landscape artists and Birmingham leaders. Auburn Urban Studio is also helping to implement the covered shed, to be built along the walking trail coming up between First and Second Avenues South and near the current site of the market. Lisa says the idea for this space is for it to be a connector, both physically and philosophically. Aside from complementing the role of the existing space by hosting farmers and vendors during cooler months, the new space can act as a meeting place, a workspace for the Pepper Place administration and additional space for chef demos and maybe even kids' activities. But taking good care of their vendors and making sure that customers are happy will always be the first priority. Lisa knows Pepper Place "is such a part of the city and so important to the lives of our farmers," she said. "They really depend on our market, and that means a lot to us. We watch this community that gathers every week.

It's like a family. The customers have a relationship with the people they buy from, our vendors get to know their customers, and it crosses racial and socioeconomic lines, age, education, we all come together." Lisa even jokes that Cathy and she compare the relationships they have with vendors and customers to having a whole lot of cousins. "We love it. It means something to us. We want to protect it, and we want it to become better every year." Without Pepper Place Farmers' Market, Birmingham might not have the successful restaurant culture it does today, with chefs focused on local ingredients picked at the peak of season, since it's difficult to imagine how much harder their jobs of sourcing these ingredients would be without the market to facilitate relationships and build bridges from farm to table.

Jones Valley Teaching Farm

Driving on the I-20/I-59 connection in Birmingham, passengers might look down on the city below and notice a strange oasis at the corner of Seventh Avenue and Twenty-fifth Street North. Tucked between a housing development and the overpass, Jones Valley Teaching Farm occupies a three-and-a-half-acre lot on which over two hundred varieties of vegetables, fruits and flowers grow. Some of these are small community garden plots, but most are in support of Jones Valley's mission to promote a healthy community through its educational efforts. Along the way, many local restaurants have taken note, and it's not uncommon to see the Jones Valley Teaching Farm name credited with ingredients on menus from small cafés to fine-dining establishments.

With seeds sewn in the early 2000s, Jones Valley began its life as a collection of small urban farms, community plots in abandoned lots and small corners of the city, due to the efforts of Edwin Marty and Page Allison, both Birmingham natives who returned home determined to start an urban farm after time at the University of California–Santa Cruz's Center for Agroecology and Sustainable Food Systems program and working in farms along the West Coast from Washington to Mexico. Farm director Katie Davis said the goal at the beginning of Jones Valley Urban Farm, the original name, wasn't initially so much about education or community involvement as it was just something Edwin had seen in other cities and believed Birmingham needed.

In 2001, the first lot was procured, a vacant lot next to an abandoned house on Tenth Avenue South in a neighborhood where the freshest food

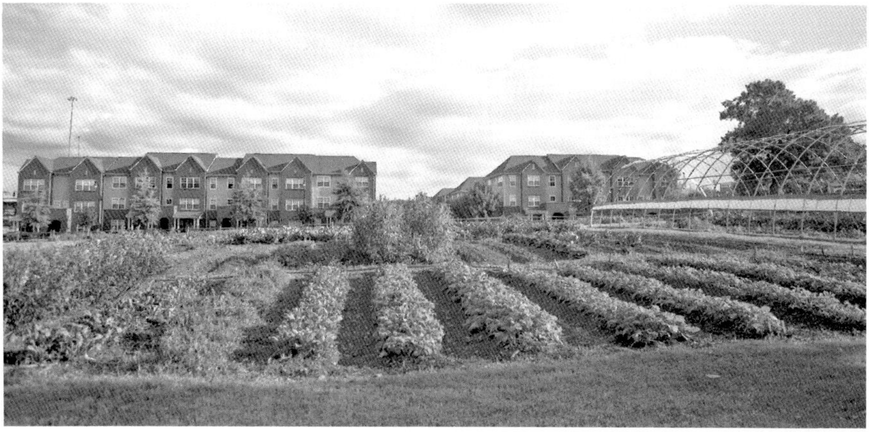

Jones Valley Teaching Farm with Hope 6 apartments in the background. *Courtesy of Jones Valley Teaching Farm; photograph by Cary Norton.*

came in plastic packages from the nearby convenience store, and Edwin and Page started farming. Both farmers had full-time day jobs in addition to running the community farm, which expanded over the next few years to include a plot in the East Avondale community and a garden on the grounds of the Alabama School of Fine Arts. Those early days were a little unfocused, according to Katie, but Edwin was drumming up attention for the farm by selling vegetables each week at Pepper Place Farmers' Market and knocking on back doors to restaurants like Frank Stitt's Highlands Bar and Grill and Chris Hastings's Hot and Hot Fish Club with his produce. The quantity and variety of those first vegetables wasn't much, but soon the quality improved and restaurants began taking notice and buying produce from Jones Valley. Along the way, Edwin had hired as program director for the farm Rachel Reinhart, the woman responsible for starting the education programs, including the partnership with the School of Fine Arts and the creation of the Seed to Plate Program, a hands-on program in which students visit the farm to learn where their food comes from and why that matters. Page and Edwin had parted ways, but the farm project had grown so much in the first few years that in 2006, the James Rushton One Foundation allowed Jones Valley access to its current site, a lot the foundation had previously used only a small portion of for its own community garden called the Garden of Hope.

That first year, a cover crop of sunflowers was planted on the grounds to improve the quality of the soil. Katie Davis remembers coming to the field of giant flowers downtown with her mother before she'd ever heard

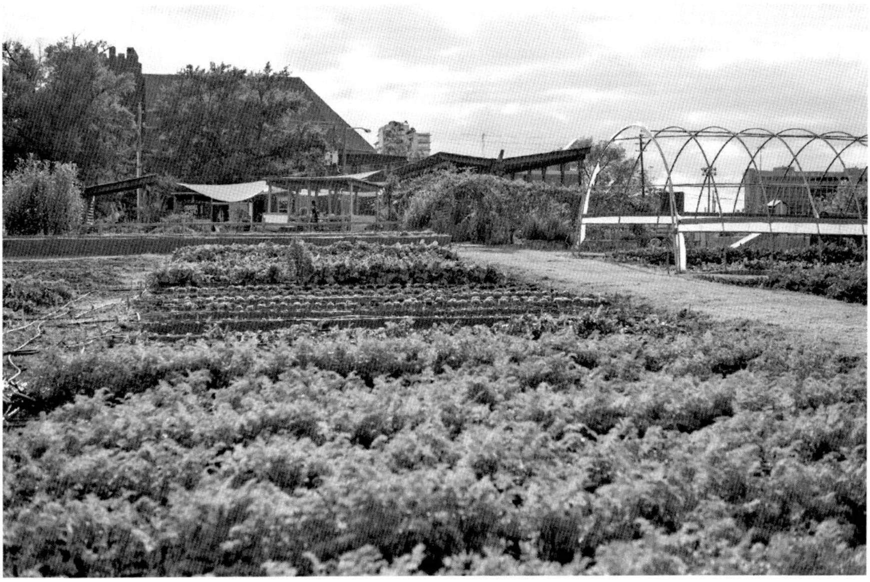

Produce grows at Jones Valley Teaching Farm. *Courtesy of Jones Valley Teaching Farm; photograph by Cary Norton.*

anything about Jones Valley. Home visiting family, Katie was on vacation from UC–Santa Cruz's Agroecology program herself, and she had no idea she'd end up back at Jones Valley just a few years later. During the fortieth anniversary of UC–Santa Cruz's Agroecology program, Katie had met Edwin, who'd come to speak at the event, and they realized not only was she working in the same position for the program that Page had previously held but she and Edwin had also spent three weeks on a twenty-foot sailboat for an Outward Bound program when Katie was a teen. They talked about the community gardens and education programs at Jones Valley, and when a job was posted on the farm's website later that year, Katie leapt at the chance to come home and join the team. "I never thought about coming back to Birmingham, really," Katie said. "But I saw that job and said, 'That's where I'm going to be.'"

In 2008, when Katie started as farm manager, she was Jones Valley's tenth to fill the position and was responsible for the diverse daily operations of the farm, which had shed the other sites and was focused on the three-and-a-half-acre plot for production and education. With just a few staff members and little funding, Katie's responsibilities included growing, harvesting, packaging, delivering, marketing and selling the produce. At that time, nearly forty restaurants filled Jones Valley's wholesale list, so the challenges included negotiating which restaurants got which produce in addition to filling orders for fifty CSA boxes each week. Fulfilling orders and spending half days delivering produce all across town taxed the small farm's capacity for production.

Edwin Marty left Jones Valley in 2011 to consult on developing urban farms in other cities, and Grant Brigham came on as executive director. One of Grant's first duties was to streamline the farm's goals and operations, refocusing its efforts toward its educational programs, including changing the name to Jones Valley Teaching Farm. Now the major operations at Jones Valley include its Good School Food program, which started at Glen Iris Elementary at the request of Principal Dr. Michael Wilson. Dr. Wilson wanted a school garden at Glen Iris, and Jones Valley helped him develop not only a garden but also a suite of educational programs for the students, their teachers and their parents. Now Good School Food is in Woodlawn Elementary, Middle and High Schools, and students manage their own farms, develop and run a weekly market where they sell their produce and learn anything from science to entrepreneurial skills in an integrated way. Through partnership with AmeriCorps, Teaching Farm Fellows are placed at each school, there every day to assist with these hands-on, investigative learning experiences. Katie believes education is "the direct route to the heart of the community and the easiest way to get in and start to implement change." Jones Valley Teaching Farm also partners with Southern Progress for its Family Kitchen program, which pairs ten families with professional chefs on site at the Southern Progress test kitchens to develop healthy recipes for the families that are economical in budget as well as time and encourage kids to help out with cooking.

As the goals of Jones Valley Teaching Farm have changed, the use of space on the farm has changed as well. Now there are thirty-eight small community garden plots that are doled out by committee and utilized by diverse groups and individuals, from neighbors in the community to people who work in big offices downtown and even people from as far away as Uganda and Germany who are now living in Birmingham. The major portion of the farm's plot is now given over to production of food designed to interest kids who come out to learn on the farm, not for the volume needed to serve forty restaurants and fifty CSAs. Planting is scheduled so there's something fresh, interesting and ripe each week, perfect for kids to pick and then turn into a quick and healthy snack with the help of instructors.

Jones Valley still does a brisk business selling to the community and a handful of restaurants though. Katie said chefs like Frank Stitt, who's always been a huge supporter of the farm and is on the board, or chefs who have traveled and tasted different varieties of produce in different places always get excited by the possibilities of their farm. They get calls weekly from restaurants wanting to offer Jones Valley produce on their menus, but with the farm's focus on education, it provides enough for only about six restaurants to consistently purchase wholesale produce. Many of those restaurants that regularly source from Jones Valley come out to the farm to pick up their produce or to check in on what's being planted and what they have to look forward to in future harvests. Luckily, the farm stand on site at the downtown farm is open daily, and cooks from restaurants like Urban Standard can stop in to shop for ingredients there instead.

Aside from sourcing from Jones Valley, Urban Standard has the distinction of being one of the first businesses in the Second Avenue North district that helped drive restaurants and bars—and the accompanying crowds—back to the area. Opened in 2007 by Tomek Wrezsien, a Polish immigrant, this coffeehouse and restaurant is the gathering place for young professionals, artists and more. From its famous cupcakes to fresh salads, soups and toasty sandwiches, often with Polish flavors, to the artisan coffee and teas, Urban Standard serves delicious meals and snacks to a bustling crowd of people from all over town. The atmosphere is distinctly European and full of quirky antiques, but there is hardly any establishment more representative of a Birmingham microcosm. Friends and co-workers run into one another without fail or planning, and the energy of the place makes it a great spot for work or just people watching.

Birmingham has changed a lot in the years since Jones Valley first broke ground, and Katie said she can see the difference in the number of young entrepreneurs who have opened up restaurants downtown near the farm. In the days when she attended city schools, going out for lunch meant choosing between a Burger King and a small Egyptian restaurant near where Café Dupont now resides. "There's a lot of growth in Birmingham," Katie said, mentioning places like El Barrio, Trattoria and Paramount. "And a lot of that growth is food." She believes the recession of the past decade brought a lot of creative professionals home to Birmingham, lured by the cheaper housing and cost of living and access to family to help with childcare, and with their return, they created or filled a demand for the style of modern, quality restaurants that are opening up around downtown. The unique atmosphere around UAB and Birmingham's medical community also gain credit from Katie for cultivating a population that is more concerned about the health of what they eat and how to improve their options. "I think

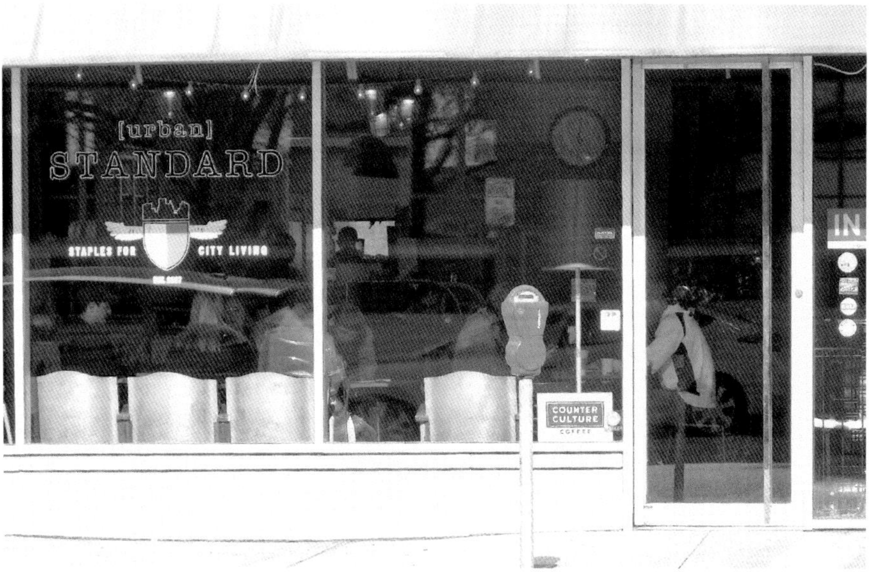

Outside Urban Standard in 2015. *Photograph by Emily Brown.*

Birmingham is one of the only places that's very optimistic right now," Katie said. And through the farm's efforts and education, hopefully that optimism is spreading to younger generations as well.

Urban Food Project

Since Frank Stitt's opening of Highlands in 1982, the farm-to-table movement in Birmingham has been slowly and steadily growing, gaining ground not just in restaurants around the city but also in the minds of people and organizations interested in affecting positive change within the city. One such group, the Urban Food Project, has been working since 2010 to improve access to fresh-from-the-farm produce, not only for restaurants interested in sourcing locally, but also in underserved populations like food deserts. Urban Food Project is a part of REV Birmingham, an economic development group in Birmingham, and has grown from a joint grant and effort between the Jefferson County Department of Health and the United Way with the initial goal of studying the city's food deserts and finding small and large ways to fill those voids, targeting obesity and affecting policy across the city.

Taylor Clark manages the Urban Food Project and has been the driving force behind its growth and focus since its inception. She found that Birmingham's food distribution infrastructure needed work if people in food deserts were to have access to fresh produce in existing corner stores and perhaps even more grocers eventually. This meant connecting farmers to markets for their fresh produce, a process that has taken time and education. Initially, Taylor helped set up new farmers' markets, like the Norwood Farmers' Market at the Trolley Stop, and she also worked to help the East Lake Farmers' Market be able to accept SNAP benefits as payment for fresh food. Then Taylor began working to set up farm-to-corner-store stands in areas without easy access to healthy food. Now three different convenience stores across the city host Urban Food Project corner store coolers, and that arm of the project has its own coordinator who helps store owners buy, sell and merchandise fresh, healthy food. Taylor says plans for 2015 include expanding into ten corner stores.

"We have limited capacity in what we can really do," Taylor said. "We've tried to grow slowly and in a really smart and intentional way and have really invested in our relationships with our growers, with our producers, and that's one of the places we've seen significant success. Without the growers and a strong network, it's all for nothing." Since the first goal of these corner stores is making healthy food choices available, some of the produce comes from commercial sources, but 85 to 90 percent of the food generally comes from the farmer network, which is truly high-quality produce. When restaurants like George Reis's Ocean and (the former) 26 source something like satsumas from the Urban Food Project for a seasonal dessert, those exact same satsumas are served in the corner markets. "That really sort of closes that divide in my mind, the accessibility gap," Taylor said. "You have [the] same access to the same healthy beautiful goods or products that George Reis is using."

The other side of the Urban Food Project is its distribution center in Woodlawn, which stores food ready to distribute to area restaurants. With the infrastructure, as well as the variety and volume of produce, already created to sell to restaurants, the project was easily able to make produce available at corner stores. For the past several years, the Urban Food Project has been borrowing a refrigerated truck from Magic City Harvest, a food recovery program in Birmingham, for its deliveries, but now a grant from the USDA has created funds for its own truck and a full-time paid driver. What started out as a small handful of restaurants, like Ted's, purchasing greens and sweet potatoes through Urban Food Project has grown to twenty-five restaurants, both high end and casual, purchasing from the network of farmers Taylor has developed. "As much as we've invested with our farmers, we've also done that with our restaurateurs," Taylor said. "We see ourselves as a liaison between the two, so we're consistently communicating to our producers what we're seeing and where the greatest opportunities are." Taylor mentioned lettuces as one example with tremendous economic opportunity for farmers, since most of the delicate lettuces restaurants prefer generally come from commercial farms in California. Getting Alabama farmers to transition to growing these varieties and harvesting them at the right time involves education in some cases. The Urban Food Project has partnered with Katie Davis of Jones Valley Teaching Farm to get her to teach workshops for farmers, established and aspiring, on how to grow some of these more delicate lettuces. "It all ties back to REV's mission of economic development," Taylor said. "There's significant economic opportunity associated with food. We all eat. It's a huge economic driver."

The Urban Food Project's list of restaurants who source from its farmers is an impressive résumé of some of Birmingham's best. Not only do meat-and-threes, like Ted's and Niki's West—famous for their vegetables—buy from the Urban Food Project, but so do some of the nicest restaurants in the city, including Hot and Hot Fish Club, Café Dupont and its casual sister Tau Poco, Little Savannah, Ocean and 26. Birmingham favorites like Silvertron in Forest Park and Rojo on Highland Avenue were early supporters of the project as well. Silvertron's owner, Marco Morosini, took over his cozy neighborhood establishment in 2007, bringing his European sensibilities and training to the menu of favorites like Alfredo pasta or the steak sandwich served with roasted vegetables. Marco said supporting local farmers came naturally to him and that he was brought up to "use what the local area around you provides." Over the hill from Silvertron, Rojo offers both casual Mexican and American food in a hip, artsy atmosphere that's famous for its broad patio where diners can watch the neighborhood foot traffic of joggers and walkers with their dogs. Rojo owners, Laney DeJonge and Clark Lopez, took over the spot of the former Highland Market in 2002 and have gained a dedicated regular clientele who come for everything from fish tacos to veggie burgers to frequent specials utilizing seasonal produce like a sweet potato burrito or peach margarita.

What's amazing about the Urban Food Project is how it gets at what connects us as people—the need to eat, the need for health and the need for options. Providing pathways for small farmers to sell the healthy food they grow to a population that needs more options and a city that is educating

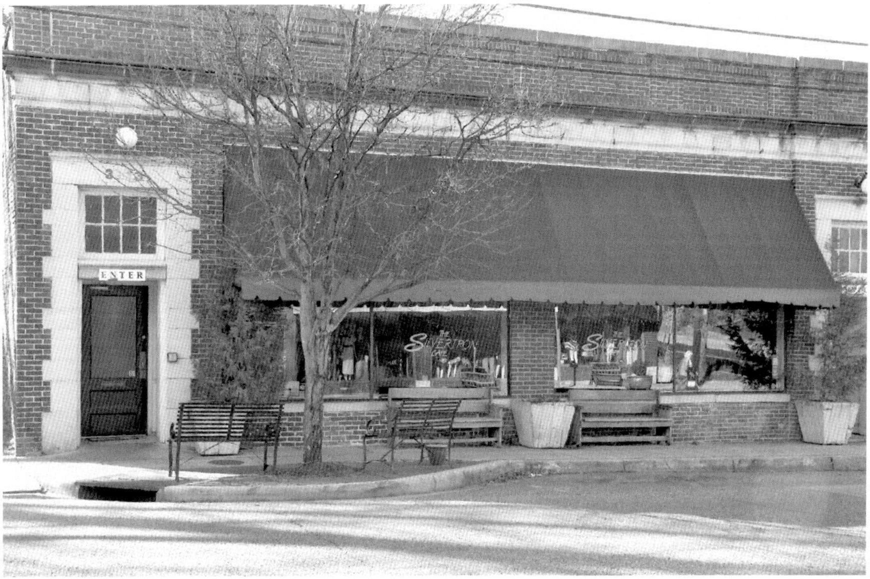

Outside Silvertron Café in 2015. *Photograph by Emily Brown.*

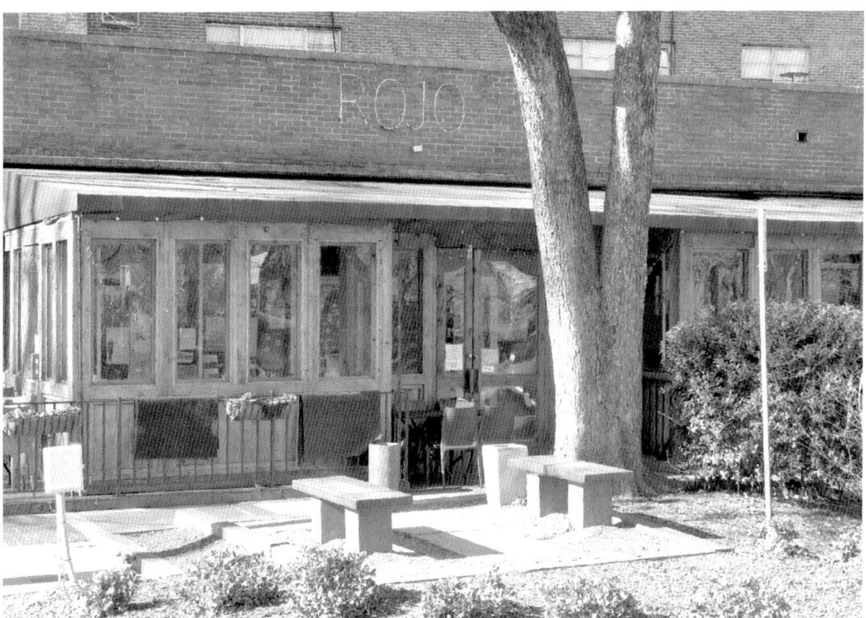

Outside Rojo in 2015. *Photograph by Emily Brown.*

itself about sustainable food systems through its restaurant menus crosses all kinds of boundaries. "We are transforming our food system to support that economic opportunity from the farm to the table," Taylor said. "We're trying to maximize that opportunity and to restructure the supply chain so we can maximize that opportunity." The hope is that eventually, even if someone can't afford to regularly eat at the white tablecloth restaurants that have been serving healthy, local food for the past few decades, the Urban Food Project's sourcing network will give plenty of opportunity for smaller, more casual places to serve the same ingredients, and food deserts will become less dry with markets full of the same produce.

Terra Preta, Snow's Bend, Owl's Hollow and Restaurant Sourcing

Several key farms have dedicated a large part of their harvests to restaurant use, and it's common to see their names in menu descriptions at a variety of restaurants around town. Two farms in particular, Terra Preta and Snow's Bend, still hold major favor with Chef Frank Stitt, which makes them in some part responsible for some of the best food around as well as for expanding the city's horizons in terms of vegetable variety. Another, Owl's Hollow, sources to multiple restaurants, from high end to casual, in addition to maintaining a key presence at Pepper Place and other farmers' markets. Plus, it has recently opened its own farm store in the suburban Bluff Park neighborhood. A picture of these three farms illustrates how serious Alabama farmers, and the restaurants who utilize their produce, are about quality food.

Terra Preta actually originated as the dream of one of Frank Stitt's employees who saw how high-quality ingredients influenced his menus. A waiter at Bottega, Michael Dean was always interested in food, but he wasn't 100 percent committed to the idea of a full-time career in food service. On Chef Stitt's suggestion, Michael started a small farm in 1996 to grow vegetables for his restaurants and, within a year, became part of the farm-to-table movement in Birmingham before there was really a movement to speak of. Other restaurants began asking for Terra Preta Farm's organic lettuces, beets, carrots, squash blossoms, herbs, tomatoes and more. By 2001, Michael's wife, Lindy, had joined his team with her background in horticulture, and their self-taught operation maintains a more prominent space in Birmingham's restaurant supply chain than its small size would suggest. They grow on only four acres, which are spread between beds in Leeds and a homestead in Vincent.

In the early days of Chef Stitt's restaurants, the only farmers' market around was the Finley Market, and Lindy said for Chef Stitt to have an "inside" guy growing for him was one of the only ways to get quality, local produce for his menus. Michael was this inside guy, and this positioning gave him ideal exposure when Chef Stitt's protégés opened restaurants of their own and needed their own local food suppliers. "If someone is interested and they don't mind hanging out until we grow enough to meet their demand," Lindy said Terra Preta will happily supply more restaurants. Terra Preta's future goals include making the homestead more fully sustainable, increasing its acreage for farming and adding a small orchard and livestock.

But the biggest change in the nearly two decades that the Deans have been the farm in the farm-to-table equation is how they've watched the popularity and accessibility of local food expand in Birmingham. "We have competition now," Lindy said. "Which is a good thing. I would say as far as the biggest change that I would notice is that a decade ago, we were supplying eight to ten restaurants. Now it's twenty to twenty-five, with more people wanting than we can provide [for] right now. More restaurants are interested in buying local. I feel like the more people are aware of local food, whether through blogs or articles or it's on the menus at restaurants or through farmers' markets like Pepper Place, the better."

Traditionally, small farmers have three outlets to sell their produce: farmers' markets, community-supported agriculture programs (CSAs) and selling to restaurants. Snow's Bend participates in all three, regularly attending Pepper Place Farmers' Market, planting and packing for a robust CSA and selling to restaurants across the state's central region. And though a lot of people complain about the younger generations not keeping up farming traditions, what's interesting about farmers like David Snow; his wife, Margaret Ann; and their farm in Coker, near Tuscaloosa, is that their education actually drove them to farming. After college, they both spent some time working on a farm in Washington State, where David got a more practical look at the lessons he'd learned in college about how food is produced in our country and where he began to think about alternative models of planting and harvesting. The season after working in Washington, David and Margaret Ann came back home to start their farm on land that had been in David's family since the 1860s. "My family has no farming background," David said. "I think the last person to use the farm in the family was my grandfather, who was sort of a gentleman farmer. He owned cattle and had somebody manage it for him. I came out to the farm my whole life and got attached to the place on the recreational side of things."

Now into its second decade, the farm has grown into a larger operation that routinely sells to restaurants like Highlands Bar and Grill, Hot and Hot Fish Club and Bettola. But it wasn't always so easy. David said it took over a year of building the farm to feel confident enough to approach restaurant chefs with their produce. "We do get some inquiries from new restaurants pretty frequently," David said. "Some work out. Some don't." For a small operation like Snow's Bend, which uses sustainable and organic practices that can be more expensive, its CSA program brings in the most profit. David and Margaret Ann can manage to farm only about 15 of the 180 available acres right now, so the CSA demands definitely come first. The strategy has been to plant double what the CSA requires, so even accounting for weather and the usual crop issues, there's enough left to source to restaurants. They make a point to plant specialty vegetables and varieties they know high-end restaurants look for. "Most of the time it's sort of us knowing about things and saying, 'Hey, I've got this neat heirloom whatever. Would you like to get some of it?'" David said. "Some chefs are very open to new stuff and experimenting and others are very traditional in stuff they like to use. It's good to have a good mix of restaurant customers. Sometimes certain ones will love only a few things. Others will like completely different things. Some things everybody likes."

The future for Snow's Bend Farm is all about growing and diversifying, with goals to add more livestock and a larger volume of vegetables, but its mission will always be to focus on consistency and reliability while honoring good land stewardship. "We're just trying to make a living and enjoy life and leave what we have in better shape than when we found it or when we started using it," David said.

Astute menu readers around Birmingham will already be familiar with the name Owl's Hollow Farm, whether from casual places like Urban Cookhouse or more high-end establishments like Little Savannah. And even if Owl's Hollow's hydroponic lettuces and tomatoes from its farm outside Gadsden haven't caught Birmingham residents' eyes on menus, its perennial presence at Pepper Place Farmers' Market, where it has participated since the market's second year, should mean consumers have heard the name.

Owner Rod Palmer describes his journey to becoming a major player in Birmingham's restaurant and farmers' market scene as "an incredible blessing." Through Owl's Hollow's participation in the Pepper Place Farmers' Market, he met many of the city's finest chefs and gained the most loyal following of customers around. When ice storms destroyed eleven years of work and the farm's greenhouses in 2011, customers came out to a benefit Urban Cookhouse hosted to support the Palmers with their prayers, cards and money, an event that ended up saving the farm. "It's overwhelming how great of an experience that terrible thing was," Rod said. "God's been freakishly good to me. Everything fell into place. When I needed my frames [for new greenhouses], someone was going out of business, so I got those frames for a fraction of what I'd have to pay. It's been real wonderful how it's all worked out." Rebuilding the farm with the benefit of knowledge gained from experience has made Owl's Hollow stronger and more efficient, so the Palmers can work smarter.

Though Rod grew up on a small five-acre farm, he went into business in residential contracting with his brother. The economic downturn sent him back to farming full time, but it was Rod's son, who began farming at age fifteen, who sparked Rod's interest in greenhouse growing. Now twenty thousand square feet of greenhouses grow organic lettuces, baby squash, tomatoes and more at Owl's Hollow. "I grow stuff now that I didn't even know what it was fifteen years ago," Rod said. "We've hit a niche market, especially with the high-end restaurants, so whatever they'll use, I'll grow." He also mentions growing hydroponic vegetables, which involves growing plants in nutrient-rich water rather than soil, attracts interest. "A lot of plant illnesses are soil born," Rod said. "So we don't have to deal with that. We put everything in the pools that lettuce needs, minus the dirt. You end up with the exact same product but healthier and with less disease." Growing and selling a healthy product are just part of Rod's values, and he firmly believes treating people well will bring good back to him and his farm: "I try to treat people the way I want to be treated, and I want to always make sure people know that I appreciate their business. And if I can make somebody happy doing that, then it makes me happy." These days, you can still catch Rod at Pepper Place and a few other markets around town, but his biggest venture is the small market he's opened up with his brother in the suburb community of Bluff Park. Fresh, seasonal produce from the farm, plus local grits, flour, soaps and more can be purchased six days a week at the store.

Urban Cookhouse

One casual café around town has gone beyond buying local produce for its restaurant to actually running farmers' markets to give its vendors and other small farmers more opportunities to sell their goods. Since the first Urban Cookhouse location in Homewood opened in 2010, owners David and Andrea Snyder have developed and grown a consistent network of farmers to source ingredients for their casual restaurant on a level unparalleled in their price point. But with a motto like "Buy Local, Eat Urban," the Snyders knew their commitment to using local produce would be what set them apart. That commitment keeps customers coming back to the now three Urban Cookhouse locations around Birmingham for a taste of their broccoli salad, strawberry lemonade or any of their other healthy sandwiches, hearty salads and fresh sides that showcase the best of Alabama fields.

Both Andrea and David grew up in Mississippi and found their way to Birmingham after college, but the idea to open a restaurant that serves the best of farmers' market–style ingredients came from a family history of a long-running and successful produce market in New Jersey run by one of the owner's great-grandfathers in the 1920s. The goal of hosting their own small market in the front of their restaurant quickly transformed into a full-fledged farmers' market in the neighborhood each week, just one of the many ways the Snyders work to support small farmers and the local economy. They've relied on help from the Urban Food Project to forge some of their key relationships with farmers, and as the Snyders' restaurant demand has grown, farmers have risen to the challenge. Andrea has said that meeting actual farmers and knowing where their food comes from is enjoyable and that "eating fresh and local is important because it creates demand for local farming and the ability for us to taste food as it should be—making food more enjoyable in its most natural form, which ultimately enhances our overall health." By 2011, Urban Cookhouse had opened a second location at the Summit, where managers at the outdoor shopping mall actually approached the Snyders about setting up a second weekly farmers' market there. Since then, the third location in Crestline opened, also with its own weekly market and customer base.

Running a booming business was always the plan, but the Snyders have remained focused on impacting local farmers and the local food economy, a goal aided by the ordering volume needed for three restaurants and a fourth that's in the works. Urban Cookhouse began working with just four farmers in 2010, but by 2014, the group had swelled to eleven farms total, with seven of those coming from the Urban Food Project network. "Now we're able to have more of an impact on local farms," Andrea said. "We're doing growers' agreements now. We're able to tell farmers exactly what we want." The growers' agreements drawn up between the restaurant and the farm are mutually beneficial—farmers can plan what to plant knowing they have a market for what they harvest, and the restaurant can plan where it orders knowing the volume will be in place. "Southern Oaks Farm in Springville is one of our main farms," Andrea said. "We went out for a tour, and they built an entire greenhouse for us for broccoli. Imagine the economic impact on those families. When we started out with one store, we bought four hundred gallons of strawberries from Harvest Farms in Cullman. We make a purée and freeze it and use it all year long for strawberry lemonade. This year we bought one thousand gallons."

Urban Cookhouse remains probably one of the best examples of how buying local produce doesn't have to translate to complicated or expensive food; it just requires hard sourcing work on the front end. Yet it's difficult to visualize how arrangements like those Urban Cookhouse has with its farmers would have even come about without the efforts of the Urban Food Project, a community of farmers familiar with the Birmingham market through Pepper Place and a customer base that appreciates the value of farm-fresh food. When you think about it, Urban Cookhouse is just the next logical step in a system that began with Frank Stitt's love of local, seasonal ingredients and his education of Birmingham residents through their coming to eat at his restaurants. Aside from keeping dollars in the local economy, sourcing local is good for the economy because buyers and patrons come to expect that same fresh quality and increase the demand for it overall. And the continuing success of Urban Cookhouse just proves that Birmingham craves that quality, even from our casual cafés.

The Pantry by Stone Hollow Farmstead

Another interesting farm-to-table spot in the suburb of Mountain Brook, the Pantry by Stone Hollow Farmstead grew as an offshoot of a goat farm known for its creamy, luscious cheeses. Owner Deborah Stone first made a name for herself around town with her signature day spa at the Colonnade. When she sold the business in 1999, Deborah wanted to return to the quieter lifestyle she'd grown up in, so she moved her family out to a small horse farm in Harpersville. Ever the busy businesswoman, Deborah soon looked for something to keep her active during the horses' breeding period, so she and her husband constructed large boxes in which to grow herbs that she could distill and use in her botanical skincare line. The goats came next, and when her family had their fill and stock of goat milk, Deborah began making cheese.

From the beginning, Deborah dedicated herself to sustainable practices at Stone Hollow Farmstead. She chose white oak and organic seeds for her herb boxes and went the extra mile with gravel and fill dirt to ensure the herbs wouldn't be contaminated with any seepage. Goats got the same ecologically conscious treatment with a special GMO-free corn feed and a rule that no goats on antibiotics would be allowed on the milking line. Feeding and caring for the animals in this careful way means they produce less milk than commercial goats, but the quality and flavor reflect this intention to craft an artisanal product.

Now Deborah also runs the Pantry as an extension of the farm and as an additional place to sell her cheeses and preserves, as well as fresh-pressed juices, raw and cooked soups and more for lunch. The ingredients for the menu come, in part, from Deborah's farm, but she also leans on other farmers, including the Urban Food Project network. Deborah has said she loves this aspect of her job. "My philosophy is to be true, to be honest, and to highlight others' efforts, other farmers' efforts, other people's efforts to deliver a quality product and to acknowledge others that have come before you and have helped you," she said.

Freshfully

Starting in 2011, Birmingham residents had the opportunity to purchase local produce and more on the Internet from a business called Freshfully. The idea was to make locally grown and raised produce and meat, along with various other local food products like grits, salsa and relishes, more readily available to area residents. Founders Jen Barnett and Sam Brasseale won the startup money as well as website development help from a local business incubation contest and set to work cultivating a network of farmers and food purveyors who would sell their goods through Freshfully's website. In addition to creating a unique shopping experience in which customers could order weekly veggie boxes for pickup at various locations around town, Freshfully's goals were to support its farmers with profits that were better than grocery stores'—86 percent of sales went directly back to the farmers—and provide a venue for sales that was easier than hauling produce to multiple farmers' markets. Freshfully's website also offered profiles on farmers and purveyors in an effort to strengthen the relationship between customers and the people responsible for growing their food.

Another contest win landed Jen, Sam and Freshfully a brick-and-mortar store, which they opened in mid-2012 across the street from Avondale Brewing Company on Forty-first Street and Second Avenue South. The market expanded the range of what Freshfully could offer, though ripe Alabama tomatoes remained a popular favorite. The store was popular in the underserved neighborhood of Avondale as well as with customers from across the city who would make special trips to pick up Alabama beef or catfish, fresh and organic squash and kale, organic milk and cream, granola and other baked goods, Alabama-made spices and sauces and even rice and beans grown in the state. Some customers even came from area restaurants where their purchases from Freshfully would show up on that week's menus. In early 2013, the store underwent renovations to allow Jen and Sam to open up a café that served fresh fruit and vegetable smoothies, sandwiches like the BLT with Alabama tomatoes and the famous Benton's bacon and hearty healthy salads, plus coffee from local roasters like Woody Wiginton of FinerGrind.

In October 2013, Freshfully expanded once again as part of REV Birmingham's REVIVE Birmingham pop-up project, opening a second location in the heart of downtown. Sadly, declining sales and uncertain crop production forced Freshfully's closure in January 2014, but the vacuum left in local food purchasing options has been sorely felt. Freshfully was known for its owners' friendliness and wholehearted support of Alabama-grown and made products, and the fact that it offered so much variety is proof of how far support of the city's local food scene has come since the early 1980s. Jen Barnett has since opened Bottle and Bone, a restaurant and butcher shop in the city's Uptown entertainment district, where, in addition to local produce in their salads and sides, customers can order and enjoy Alabama Wagyu beef, local beer and more for lunch, dinner or to take home and prepare in their own kitchens. By continuing to support local ranchers, farmers and brewers, but in a more focused setting, Jen is filling a need for artisanal products showcasing the best of the state's products prepared by some of the city's most talented craftsmen, something Frank Stitt himself mentioned the city needs.

8

THE FUTURE OF BIRMINGHAM'S FOOD SCENE BEYOND THE CITY

Birmingham residents are nothing if not supportive of their native sons and daughters. We're a city in the midst of rebirth and redefinition, in large part because of the quality and variety of our restaurant scene. New places open up downtown, chefs revamp old favorites to stay current and a booming craft beer and cocktail scene make a noteworthy food culture even more vibrant. Even our casual lunch spots and a homegrown popsicle business are making waves beyond the city. Birmingham has a lot to celebrate and a lot to be thankful for, especially now that the secret is out about what honest, inventive, healthy and thoughtful food and drinks our people create every day.

Trattoria Centrale/El Barrio/Paramount

At the forefront of Birmingham's quality fast-casual scene is a group of restaurateurs with both an excellent résumé and a desire to keep things fresh and lively in the growing revitalization of downtown. Brian Somershield and his partner Geoff Lockert opened their first restaurant, a pizza place called Trattoria Centrale, on Twentieth Street in 2009, and during their first five years in business, they've added two other wildly successful and different restaurants and three partners along the way, all of which has paved the way for even more restaurants and bars to open up nearby.

Both Brian and Geoff are originally from Cleveland. They've been friends since college, and both got their first exposure to fine dining by waiting tables at one of the better restaurants in their hometown. Brian said he was actually kind of a picky eater as a kid and never really thought about food in any significant way until the thoughtful preparation and presentation of meals at that restaurant opened his eyes to the creativity of food and made him curious to try making it himself. Working his way through the front of the house at various restaurants, usually with Geoff, Brian eventually decided he wanted to attend culinary school, and a fateful golfing trip to Birmingham before starting school introduced him to Chef Frank Stitt and Highlands Bar and Grill, thanks to a recommendation his uncle gave him about where to eat. "Obviously the food was great southern food, something I hadn't had a lot of exposure to," Brian said. "What blew me away was the service, which I hadn't experienced before. It was gracious. It was impeccable, everything that's great about the South wrapped up in a dining experience. That's what really stuck with me." So when looking for a culinary school internship, Brian applied at Highlands and landed a spot. He loved the work and the restaurant so much that at the end of his four-month stint he sat down with Chef Stitt and asked if he could come back after culinary school graduation. Chef Stitt assured him he'd find a place for him—if not at Highlands, then at one of his other three restaurants—and after graduation Brian came back to Birmingham and Highlands, eventually working his way up and over to the chef de cuisine position at Chez Fonfon, where he stayed for three years.

Back in college, Brian and Geoff had always talked about opening some sort of business together, maybe a bagel shop like Geoff had seen and fallen in love with or maybe another type of restaurant. So when Brian was settled in Birmingham, married and ready to go out on his own, he and Geoff began talking more seriously about opening their own restaurant. The partners looked at places both in Cleveland and in Birmingham but ultimately decided that the cache of having worked with Frank Stitt would be the best advantage they could have in starting a new restaurant. Brian said that having his name associated with Chef Stitt "goes a long way, but you have to sustain that with your own work and your own talent. We were terrified of what we were about to do, but we found the little spot downtown and thought we could fill a niche." Trattoria Centrale has a very European feel to its narrow space, but the ingredients that top the fresh pizzas and fill the breakfast frittatas are all local. Being known for quality pizza and an excellent Sunday brunch has made Trattoria a favorite among the downtown lunch crowd as well as other locals who make the trip downtown just for their food.

By 2011, Brian and Geoff were ready to start a second venture, and when they found a spot in the reawakening Second Avenue North district, they knew it would be perfect for their take on Mexican: El Barrio. But since they were already working hard at one restaurant, and their priorities included wanting to have lives and families outside the restaurants, Brian and Geoff decided to find partners to help them run the new place. Chris Cullen, a friend of Geoff's from Ohio, came on to run the front of the house, and a loyal customer at Trattoria led them to Neville Baay, a chef who'd been working as a private cook and who could run the kitchen for them. Brian jokes about making Neville audition for them and says they invited him and his family to Chris and Geoff's apartment to cook for them all before deciding on hiring him. "I'm sure it was nerve wracking," Brian said. But the group clicked and has formed a flourishing partnership at their Mexican-inspired place that almost always has a wait on weekends. Patrons can enjoy the hand-painted mural and rough wood paneling in the restaurant while sipping a spicy margarita or paloma at the bar while they wait for goodies like fresh ceviche, pork or vegetarian tacos or even a signature meatloaf entrée cooked with Mexican flavors. And just like at Trattoria, local farmers' ingredients are the stars of El Barrio's menu.

For their third concept, Brian, Geoff, Chris and Neville took on a fifth partner, Ben Smith, a bartender Brian knew from Chez Fonfon who'd been helpful in finding the spot for Trattoria. Back in 2009, Ben had wanted to open his own bar and had been looking at a spot on the corner of Twentieth Street and Second Avenue North. That venture didn't work out for Ben, but when the Trattoria guys were ready to open their own bar, full of arcade games and serving creative pub fare, they felt it was only fitting to open in that same spot, with Ben as their new partner. Paramount opened in 2014 and serves as a great spot to grab drinks with friends, show off pool-playing skills and enjoy creative takes on hot dogs, burgers and appetizers like Alabama peanut hummus.

Brian said the path his career has taken and the successes they've seen have all been due to great timing and luck in finding people they could trust to work just as hard and care just as much as he and Geoff have since the beginning:

> *Geoff and I get a lot of credit for what we've done with our restaurants, but we couldn't have done it without the help of Chris, Neville and Ben. They're very important parts. One of the things we learned from Frank and*

Chris is it's very easy to get married to your profession. You can't ever let up, or you become not relevant. Frank is there every day. He keeps it relevant. Geoff and I find that important but didn't really want to be married to our work forever, so bringing on partners helps. It allows for me to be home on a Saturday. That's my family day. Neville and Chris get Sundays with their families. We have restaurant schedules, but they're good. It's very important to us that we have balance. We are more than willing to sacrifice potential revenue for quality of life that is hard to attain in this business.

Brian recognizes that he and his partners get credit for being catalysts for economic growth and restaurant traffic downtown, opening the way for more restaurants and bars to join in the scene, but he points out that without the pioneering efforts of Chris Dupont, who opened his high-end Café Dupont on Twentieth Street when nothing else was around, and Urban Standard on Second Avenue North, which brought the young, hip crowd back to the area, they might not have been so successful themselves. "I think part of it," Brian said, "Being that we're not from here we didn't realize the negative stigma that came with downtown." But by opening three new restaurants in five years, Brian and his partners are part of the movement that's bringing life and activity back to downtown. He loves seeing new places open and believes there's plenty of space for more. More diversity in terms of world cuisine is one of the only things Brian thinks downtown Birmingham is lacking to have a better food scene:

I think we're headed in the right direction. People are serving high-quality things stripped away from the perceived pretention. I don't think fine dining is pretentious. I think young guys like us and Mauricio and the guys over at Hotbox are taking their fine-dining training and saying, 'This food is great, and my training is great, and I want to do that and do something a little more casual.' I think that's a nationwide thing. You can get really great food, and you don't have to dress up for it.

Brick and Tin

With a pedigree that includes time spent at Bottega, as sous chef at Hot and Hot and as chef de cuisine at Highlands, it might seem surprising that Mauricio Papapietro decided to open a casual lunch restaurant focusing on sandwiches and soups. But in 2010, when he opened Brick and Tin in a spot on Twentieth Street and named it for the architectural details exposed during renovation, Mauricio was both riding and helping create a wave of fast-casual dining options in Birmingham that owe the quality of their food to a fine-dining lineage like his own. Lunch from a menu that includes sandwiches on bread baked fresh on site and filled with a seasonally changing mix of locally sourced produce, artisan cheeses and more costs only around ten dollars, and those ingredients are often the same varieties, from the same farms, as you'll find on Chef Stitt and Chef Hastings's tables.

Mauricio found his way to his style of honest, thoughtful cooking almost by accident, though he credits his mother's cooking with setting the foundation of appreciation for really good food. As a recent graduate of Sewanee in history, Mauricio moved back home to Birmingham and tried to figure out what he wanted to do with his life. The food he ate at the time wasn't the best, and he remembered how his mother used to prepare Italian and South American specialties with such care and love. Mauricio says he became "obsessed" with cooking and began trying to learn as much as he could about technique, even reading textbooks for both the Culinary Institute of America and Le Cordon Bleu cooking schools. Figuring if he was going to get hands-on learning, he should go to the best, Mauricio then went to Bottega in 2002 and asked for a job; he was hired on the prep line. Working his way up, Mauricio took a year off to work and learn in Italy—both his parents are Italian, though they lived in Chile for a long time before he was born—and then returned to Birmingham to work at Hot and Hot. A few years working his way up the chain under Chef Hastings gave Mauricio lots of experience with local farmers and managing costs in a kitchen, and then he transitioned back to working under Chef Stitt at Highlands, eventually landing as chef there, taking in all the lessons Chef Stitt had to offer, as well. "For me, it was kind of a late thing," Mauricio said. "After I'd gone to school and everything I just got into it and got the bug and learned in the best restaurants in Birmingham."

Deciding to go out on his own and open a restaurant involved a lot of time and planning. Mauricio had even considered finding a space of his own downtown in between working at Hot and Hot and Highlands but decided he wasn't ready yet. "It's really hard work," Mauricio said. "I thought if I'm going to work this hard, I'm going to do it for myself." Choosing downtown for the location of his first restaurant seemed like a good idea because of the built-in clientele of doctors, lawyers and other businesspeople working in the area. "I learned from the best here, from Frank, about white tablecloth fine dining, which I think is the highest level of cooking you can do, in terms of technique and all the traditional things you learn," Mauricio said. "I wanted to bring it into a more accessible format, an everyday format, a cheaper format where people can do it a couple times of week or you don't have to be making a lot of money to eat [at] a place and get really good quality food that's prepared with care." Plus, being in his early thirties, Mauricio knew he wanted to start a family, something difficult to do if you're working long hours and at night. "It was a personal decision," said Mauricio. "But also I was trying to think of ways to bring all of that training into an everyday format, so the sandwich was the idea for me."

With the downtown crowd coming in regularly for lunches of seasonal sandwiches and soups and Friday dinners of more hearty fare, Mauricio decided to open a second location in Mountain Brook for both lunch and dinner, six days a week, in early 2014. With two restaurants to buy for, Mauricio is happy to be able to support in a more significant way local farmers, some of whom are his friends, like David Snow, who went to Sewanee with him. "We can buy three hundred pounds of heirloom tomatoes in the summer, every week," Mauricio said. But buying produce from local, organic farms comes at a higher price, and with the affordable meals he offers at Brick and Tin, Mauricio has learned to be creative and smart in how he utilizes his ingredients. Aside from David Snow, Brick and Tin also sources from Trent Boyd in Cullman, another friend of Mauricio's; Michael Dean of Terra Preta; and a handful of others. "It's really important for me to buy as much stuff from them as I can, so a lot of times we actually design our menus based on what they have," Mauricio said. "I've worked really hard to get to where I am, and…these farmers are some of the only people I know who work as much or more as I do. They work so hard all the time, and…it's kind of unrelenting work, so I have a lot of respect for what they do, too."

Respect for food, respect for the ingredients and respect for relationships are all at the core of what Brick and Tin represents—values you'll find at white tablecloth restaurants around town as well. One of those relationships illustrates how special, talented and supportive Birmingham's food community really is. Back when Mauricio worked as chef de cuisine at Highlands, he became friends with Brian Somershield of Trattoria Centrale, who was working as chef de cuisine at Chez Fonfon at the same time. "We were both working really hard for somebody we both really respected, learning a lot," Mauricio said. "I have great respect for Brian. He's savvy, he's really smart, sharp, talented, quick-witted, and he's always been that way. He's just a solid good person, and he's honest." Both chefs had the desire to go out on their own, and Mauricio jokes that Brian just beat him to the punch with his dream of opening a casual spot downtown. "The spot I found happened to be right across the street from him, and so we talked, and he was always really gracious," Mauricio said. "I think he knew, like I know, this is really a burgeoning, growing scene down there, and there's enough people for there to be more restaurants. And he also believes, like I do, that the more restaurants there are down there, the better it is for everybody." Mauricio's dream is that Birmingham's downtown revitalization will continue and eventually become a place with a more vibrant, walkable nightlife, full of lots of great dining options. "I hope that we can be a catalyst for bringing that high level of food and that new type of business, which is really trying to pull from the local land," Mauricio said. He'd like Brick and Tin "to be a catalyst for more casual places, so there can be more places that you can eat that have good quality food every day." For his part, Brian says Mauricio is "a great cook and a great guy. I think we share a lot of the same principles." Having another restaurant across the street, especially one the other likes and respects so much, makes doing business easier as well. Brian said at least once a week someone is running over to borrow dill or some other fresh ingredient, which just adds to the atmosphere of camaraderie and desire for mutual success that's grown in the downtown scene.

Food Trucks

As proof that Birmingham really is riding the wave of top-notch foodie culture, we even have a full variety of food trucks that have hit the scene in the past few years. These mobile restaurants run the gamut from simple tacos, pizza, barbecue and burgers to the exotic flavors of a Vietnamese báhn mì, spicy fried shrimp po'boy or beyond-definition steamed buns filled with everything from catfish to pork belly. We even have a food truck, Melt, devoted to wildly inventive riffs on grilled cheese, including one with meatloaf nestled inside the melted cheese. Throughout the year several festivals and events celebrate this vibrant food truck scene and gather them together in one spot, such as Railroad Park, for an afternoon and evening dedicated to them showcasing their best. Many of the trucks have regular routes in downtown and the suburbs so that, depending on the day of the week, nearby officeworkers can grab a special lunch just outside their buildings or brewery patrons can grab a bite to go with their happy hour pint. Most importantly though, these food trucks are just as committed to quality and service as their more traditional counterparts, and several even come with a high-end restaurant pedigree.

Ask anyone which is the best food truck around Birmingham, and more likely than not their answer will be Shindigs. Known for their beyond basic burgers, truffle fries, steamed buns and more, Mac Russell and Chad Schofield of Shindigs made a pledge early on to follow their motto, "Farm to Fork." And it's not surprising these two believe local sourcing is the best way to put out a consistently top-notch product, since both worked under Chef Chris Hastings as well as Clif and Maureen Holt of Little Savannah, two places where farm-to-table dining is standard. Mac even grew up on a ranch in central Alabama that raised Hereford cattle, and that strong connection to food sourcing stayed with him as he rose through the ranks at various restaurants and at culinary school with Chad. "It's all about trying to be honest in the whole process," said Mac. "We're human. We get grass fed, but we're not raising them all. It isn't perfect. We want to be able to grow it all…I want to be able to produce it all and have that stay in Alabama."

Shindigs began in 2011 as a catering company. Mac and Chad had catered a wedding for a friend at Ross Bridge Hotel and Resort, and after the great success of the event, they looked at each other and realized they might have a good business together. The food truck came about as a catering tool, and the business is still about 80 percent traditional catering. Mac says the truck is fun and has been a creative outlet for them. "We're just using our technique and training or using a lower cut," Mac said. "It's easy to make filet tender, but it's more fun to do something exciting with other stuff you can pay less for."

Catering events as exclusive as Frank Stitt's holiday party as well as serving burgers to hungry lunchers might make less committed restaurateurs forgo their principles, but Mac says sustainability and being good stewards are at the core of their business. He credits their time watching Chef Hastings and others develop relationships with farmers and ranchers with the relative ease they've had doing the same for their own business. But being in the business for the right reasons has also guided Shindigs' success. "Now when we're doing fast food off the truck or whether it's fine dining, it's so much easier to get those products and so much easier to accomplish sustainable practices, which is great for the community," Mac said. "That's why we started Shindigs." Beyond looking for fame or fortune, Mac and Chad are concerned with their long-term goals of wanting to create their own fully sustainable network where they're responsible for growing or raising what they need for the catering and food truck as well as have their own event space or restaurant or both as an outlet for their food. Mac says they'd like to get to the point where they can employ and influence enough people to change the mentality about food citywide, so everyone believes sustainable is best.

Mac believes he and Chad have been blessed throughout the growth of their business, and he stresses that they try to stay unselfish, focusing on doing things the right way, even if they only break even, until they can grow enough to make a profit for everybody involved. Part of their blessing has been the response from Birmingham residents, who have grown to recognize quality eats when they see them. "I think we're blessed for our size," Mac said of Birmingham. "I hate when people say it's better in Atlanta because it shows they don't know…I think for our size it's as good as it needs to be, and it can only continue to get better because of the popularity." The city's popularity brought Andrew Zimmern for a visit in 2012 with his show *Bizarre Foods America*, and one of his stops was Shindigs. "It was fun to see how much people like it," Mac said. The Shindigs guys keep a fun and fresh presence on social media, which is just one more part of how they're ushering the future into Birmingham's food scene.

Two other popular food trucks originated as off shoots of restaurants around town: Slice Pizza and Brew and Cantina Tortilla Grill. Like Shindigs, they also work as catering tools for the brick-and-mortar establishments and can regularly be found at festivals and events across the city. And while these food trucks are most certainly supported by their restaurants, they both deserve a mention specifically for themselves because the quality and consistency of the food never waivers on the road.

Slice Pizza and Brew and its accompanying food truck began as the brainchild of brothers Jason, Chris and Jeff Bajalieh. Like a lot of Birmingham restaurateurs, the Bajalieh brothers grew up in the restaurant business, watching their father, aunts and uncles and picking up tricks of the trade. When the space in Lakeview came up, they knew they wanted to open a restaurant combining two American favorites: pizza and beer. The choice to use local ingredients and feature local brews was a natural one when they started to look for the best sources, and this choice has made them a favorite for everyone from families to friends on a night out. Slice is a big customer of the Urban Food Project, which Jason said has taken a lot off their plate in terms of the responsibility of tracking down farmers. But the brothers also regularly source from Owl's Hollow and use Alabama-made products like Wickles Pickles and both Pilleteri and Conecuh sausage. One of their most popular and unusual pizzas, the Soul Pie, is topped with local turnip greens, Conecuh sausage and black-eyed peas. All Slice's specialty pizzas on their menu come with pairing suggestions for complementary brews from places like Good People Brewing, Cahaba Brewing, Avondale Brewing Company and Trim Tab Brewing—all local guys, too. The advent of the Slice truck came from catering demand for parties and events. The restaurant, though equipped with a wide and inviting patio outside the quirky building, isn't large enough for big parties, so the truck allows them to serve more customers as well as participate in the city's food truck events or be available for many of the charity events they host and support. "We're really big on community outreach," Jason said. "Without the locals in the community, we don't have any business. You should support the people who support you. We try to preach experience. It's not about just the food and atmosphere, it's about the total experience."

Cantina on Wheels, the mobile arm of legendary Birmingham restaurateur Guillermo Castro's Cantina Tortilla Grill, bills itself as the city's first and only gourmet taquería. Since Guillermo's passing in 2011, his brother Jorge has run the restaurant and truck, which are known for their fish and vegetarian tacos as well as amazingly tasty fries. The truck is often parked downtown to serve the UAB crowd during lunch or near the restaurant in Lakeview for late-night eats. With Cantina, Guillermo expanded his already popular restaurant mini empire in Birmingham. In 1997, when he opened his first restaurant, Sol y Luna, he was one of the first places to serve flavors from his native Guadalajara, plus an extensive tequila list, in an upscale manner. For a while, Guillermo operated another restaurant next door to Sol y Luna, called Los Angeles, which expanded on his style, and in 2003, he opened Cantina as a place to showcase the flavors of street food, like tacos, from around Latin America and beyond. Sadly, Los Angeles and Sol y Luna are no more, but at least with Cantina and Cantina on Wheels, the legacy Guillermo built lives on in fresh and exciting flavors.

Birmingham-Based Businesses Moving Beyond the City

As further proof that Birmingham really is an amazing food town, several of our homegrown businesses have developed franchise locations that have moved beyond the city and even beyond the state. Word is getting out that good food comes from Birmingham, and those other cities want a taste of it for themselves. Aside from Golden Rule and Jim 'N Nick's, which have shared their Birmingham brands of barbecue around the Southeast, two small businesses in particular are bringing their Birmingham flavors to a whole new audience. Zoe's Kitchen, a small café with a lineage stretching back to fine dining at John's Restaurant, and Steel City Pops, a popsicle joint that offers the freshest seasonal flavors in craft popsicles, represent their hometown in a way that makes us proud.

Zoe's Kitchen began as a way for Zoe Cassimus, daughter of John's Restaurant's originator John Proferis, to share her love of healthy, simple Greek cooking with friends. Her mother's style of cooking—nothing fried, not a lot of sugar but lots of healthy flavoring from olive oil and other Mediterranean ingredients—heavily influenced Zoe's own cooking philosophy, and when she opened the first Zoe's Kitchen in Homewood in 1995, she developed the menu to reflect the lighter side of Greek cuisine. Popular items at the casual spot include the chicken salad, which is chock-full of freshly cooked chicken; pita sandwiches stuffed with things like lean turkey meat and the signature vinegar-based slaw; and chicken roll-ups served with salsa for dipping. Zoe's son, John, encouraged her to franchise the business, and soon several other locations opened around Birmingham. Zoe's Kitchens remain popular not just because of their great-tasting food but also because families could get a really reasonably priced meal in a casual and comfortable setting. Many people also love the restaurant because of its focus on nutrition, and all the nutritional information for Zoe's menus can be found on its website. By early 2014, Zoe's Kitchens were in fifteen states at 111 locations, with plans to open nearly 30 more by the end of the year. Zoe Cassimus and her son, John, eventually sold the chain, so it's no longer Birmingham based. But Zoe's Kitchens' Birmingham-influenced roots will continue to be appreciated as the franchise expands across the country with its authentic Greek flavors.

What's impressive about Steel City Pops is owner Jim Watkins's dedication to using seasonal ingredients to flavor his unique brand of popsicles, or paletas, that have created a craving around the city for these cool, creamy, icy treats. Watkins started his craft popsicle store in 2012 after being inspired by his family's visit to a similar place in Nashville over a decade earlier. "I thought I'd like to do something like that—fresh, creative," Jim said. "I don't have a culinary degree, but this was something I felt like I could get my hands around and be able to develop." With help from his mother developing recipes and support from his wife and sons, Jim worked hard to create this vibrant business that has expanded beyond the initial store and mobile cart that regularly appears at Pepper Place Farmers' Market to four other locations around Birmingham and two in Texas. Popular flavors of Steel City Pops include everything from exotic Strawberry Balsamic, Chocolate Chili and Avocado in the summer to Poached Pear, Maple Bacon with Bourbon and Buttermilk in the fall. Of course, it also offers simple flavors of chocolate, vanilla, lime, strawberry and more, but whether you're choosing wild or tame, the freshness and the quality of the ingredients that go into making these pops are what makes them irresistible. "Something will catch my eye when I'm looking at good produce," Jim said. "I'll see beautiful raspberries, and I'll want to use them. Citrus pairs naturally, and it's a natural preservative as well. We use a lot of lime, lemon, and orange juice that's all fresh squeezed here." Jim has made using organic and local products as much as possible a major characteristic of Steel City Pops. "I want people to be eating a lot of fruit that's sweetened with a natural product," he said. "When you look at it, it looks real. My banana pop looks like a banana, not bright yellow." This small family business has made waves in Birmingham's culinary community quickly, and it's no wonder its mass appeal on a craft scale has inspired its expansion beyond our city.

Celebrating the City: Birmingham Restaurant Week

Birmingham residents are nothing if not supportive of our vibrant restaurant scene. Without our locals and their word-of-mouth selling or our wide appetites and appreciation for variety and quality, the restaurant culture wouldn't be where it is today. We're proud of our restaurants' successes, and we like to take friends and visitors out to dine to show off the best and the brightest. Out of this love of good local food, and a desire to bring more spotlight on our growing reputation, James Little of REV Birmingham, an economic development group, began Birmingham Restaurant Week in 2010. Each August, participating restaurants, which numbered nearly fifty in 2014, offer special fixed-price menus for the ten-day event. Diners can get lunch for five dollars at a place like Ted's Restaurant or dinner for thirty dollars at Chef Frank Stitt's Highlands Bar and Grill or Bottega, as well as lunch and dinner at various price points in between. Menus range from traditional southern fare to inspired seasonal specialties and give customers a chance to try places they might not normally splurge for as well as revisit favorites to see what's new.

New places open all the time, many with already well-known talent behind them, and Birmingham is headed toward status as a major foodie destination town. Zagat even named Birmingham its number-one Next Hot Food City in America in 2015. Service and hospitality are the backbone of many Birmingham restaurants and represent that special quality beyond impeccable food that keeps customers coming back again and again. Far from our origins as a town of steaks and seafood, Birmingham has imagination and drive and is filled with people who want everyone to succeed. Community and family have always been at the heart of Birmingham's restaurant culture. It takes a special breed of people, people who love feeding other people and sharing their creative passion, to join that community and drive it into the future.

BIBLIOGRAPHY

For more information about most of the restaurants mentioned in this book, or to plan your next meal out in Birmingham, please see this list of websites.

Bettola: http://www.opentable.com/bettola-birmingham
Big Bad Breakfast: http://www.urbanspoon.comr/45/1852180/restaurant/Hoover/Big-Bad-Breakfast-Birmingham
Birmingham Restaurant Week: http://bhamrestaurantweek.com
Bottega: http://bottegarestaurant.com
Bottle and Bone: http://www.bottleandbone.com
Brick and Tin: http://www.brickandtin.com
The Bright Star: http://thebrightstar.com
Café Dupont: http://www.cafedupont.net
Cantina Tortilla Grill: http://cantinatortillagrill.com
Century Restaurant and Bar: http://www.centurybirmingham.com
Chez Fonfon: http://www.fonfonbham.com
Chez Lulu: http://www.chezlulu.us
Chop Suey Inn: http://chopsueyinn.net
The Club: http://www.theclubinc.org/Club/Scripts/Home/home.asp
Continental Bakery: http://www.chezlulu.us
Dales Seasoning: http://www.dalesseasoning.com.
DoDiYo's: http://dodiyos.com
Dyron's Low Country: http://www.dyronslowcountry.com
Eagle's Restaurant: http://www.eaglesrestaurant.com
80 Pops: http://www.homewoodgourmet.com
El Barrio: http://elbarriobirmingham.com
Ferocious Dogs: https://www.facebook.compages/Ferocious-Dogs/370915066358480
The Fish Market Restaurant: http://thefishmarket.net
G-Dog's and Gyros: http://www.gdogshotdogs.com
Golden Rule Bar-B-Q: http://www.goldenrulebbq.biz

Great Wall Chinese Restaurant: http://www.greatwallbirmingham.com
Green Acres Café: http://www.greenacres-cafe.com
Gus's Hot Dogs: http://www.urbanspoon.comcities/45-birminghamrestaurants/490441-gus-s-hot-dogs/menu
Highlands Bar and Grill: http://www.highlandsbarandgrill.com
Homewood Gourmet: http://www.homewoodgourmet.com
Hot and Hot Fish Club: http://www.hotandhotfishclub.com
Hotbox: http://www.hotboxbirmingham.com
Jim 'N Nick's: http://www.jimnnicks.com
John's City Diner: http://www.johnscitydiner.com
Little Savannah: http://littlesavannah.com
Melt: http://www.meltbham.com
Michael's Restaurant: http://www.michaelstheoriginal.com
Niki's: http://www.urbanspoon.comr/45/490759/restaurant/Downtown/Nikis-Birmingham
Niki's West: http://www.nikiswest.com
Ocean/26: http://oceanbirmingham.com
Ollie Irene: http://www.ollieirene.com
The Pantry by Stone Hollow Farmstead: http://www.stonehollowfarmstead.com
Paramount: http://www.paramountbirmingham.com
Pepper Place Market: http://www.pepperplacemarket.com.
Rojo: http://rojobirmingham.com
Saw's: http://www.sawsbbq.com
Shindings: http://www.shindigscateringtrucks.com
Silvertron: http://www.silvertroncafe.us
Slice Pizza and Brew: http://slicebirmingham.com
Smokehouse Seafood and Steak: http://www.urbanspoon.comr/45/491000/restaurant/Pratt/Smokehouse-Steak-Seafood-Birmingham
Sneaky Pete's: http://www.sneakypeteshotdogs.com
Steel City Pops: http://steelcitypops.com
Tau Poco: http://www.taupoco.com
Ted's Restaurant: http://tedsbirmingham.com
Trattoria Centrale: http://trattoriacentrale.com
Urban Cookhouse: http://urbancookhouse.com
Urban Food Project: http://www.revbirmingham.org/rev-biz/the-urban-food-project
Urban Standard: http://urbanstandard.net
Zoe's Kitchen: http://zoeskitchen.com

Sources

Angell, Glory Clark. *Birmingham Inside Out.* N.p.: self-published, 1983, 143–71.
Bajalieh, Jason. Phone interview, April 18, 2014.
Beasley, Lisa. Phone interviews, January 2013 and December 9, 2014.
Birmingham Age Herald. "G.J. Jebeles Began His Rise with an Eatery in Nashville." March 17, 1944.

———. November 1905.

Birmingham Business Journal. "Ollie's BBQ Closes, but the Sauce Will Live On." June 28, 1999. http://www.bizjournals.combirminghamstories/1999/06/28/story7.html.

Birmingham News. "Gus J. Jebeles, Former Owner of Barons, Dies." November 6, 1960.

The Bright Star family with Niki Sepsas. *A Centennial Celebration of the Bright Star Restaurant*. Tuscaloosa: University of Alabama Press, 2007.

Brownell, Blaine A. "Birmingham, Alabama: New South City in the 1920s." *Journal of Southern History* 38 (1972): 21–48.

Calvert, Lawrence. Phone interview, October 31, 2014.

Carlton, Bob. "Birmingham Restaurateur Guillermo Castro, Who Owned Sol Y Luna and Cantina, Dies at 52." Al.com. http://blog.al.combob-carlton/2011/07/birmingham_restaurateur_guille.html.

———. "G-Dogs and Gyros Hot Dog Shop Is the Latest Dining Venture for Birmingham's Matsos Family." Al.com. http://www.al.comentertainment/index.ssf/2012/01/g-dogs_gyros_is_the_latest_res.html.

———. "Highlands Bar and Grill's Hall of Chefs: A Photo Gallery of Birmingham's Top Culinary Talent." Al.com. http://www.al.comentertainment/index.ssf/2014/05/highlands_hall_of_chefs_a_whos.html#incart_river.

———. "Historic Cobb Lane Restaurant Set to Close on Saturday." Al.com. http://blog.al.comscenesource/2009/01/historic_cobb_lane_restaurant.htm8.l.

———. "Ted's Restaurant, a Birmingham Institution, Celebrates 40 Years in Business." Al.com. http://www.al.comentertainment/index.ssf/2013/06/teds_restaurant_a_birmingham_i.html.

Cassimus, Zoe. Interviewed by Amy Evans for the Southern Foodways Alliance, March 11, 2004.

"Charles Gratton—Birmingham Alabama." Interview for Duke University Center for Documentary Studies, October 15, 2014.

Clark, Taylor. Phone interviews, July 2013 and October 30, 2014.

Cooley, Angela Jill. "The Customer Is Always White." In *The Larder: Food Studies Methods from the American South*. Edited by John T. Edge, Elizabeth S.D. Engelhardt and Ted Ownby. Athens: University of Georgia Press, 2013: 240–72.

Davis, Katie. In-person interview, October 22, 2014.

Dean, Lindy. Phone interview, March 2014.

DeJonge, Laney. Phone interview, September 4, 2013.

Duncan, Martie, and Chandra Temple. "Introduction." In *Birmingham's Best Bites: Favorite Recipes from Restaurants, Bars, and Food Trucks around the Magic City*. Birmingham, AL: Produced by M Content Media to benefit the Birmingham Public Library and printed by EBSCO Media, 2014.

Dupont, Chris. Phone interview, November 20, 2014.

Gratton, Greg. In-person interview, October 27, 2014.

Griffin, Carole. Phone interview, June 2012.

Hastings, Chris. Phone interview, October 29, 2014.

Hollis, Tim. "The Rest and the Restaurants." In *Memories of Downtown Birmingham: Where All the Lights Were Bright*. Charleston, SC: The History Press, 2014.

Holt, Clif. Phone interview, April 2013.

Holt, Maureen. Phone interview, November 17, 2014.

Hontzas, Betty. Interviewed by Amy Evans for the Southern Foodways Alliance, May 9, 2004.

Hontzas, Pete. Interviewed by Amy Evans for the Southern Foodways Alliance, March 9, 2004.

Keith, Todd. *Birmingham Then and Now*. London: Pavilion Books, 2014, 39–76.

———. *Insider's Guide to Birmingham*. Guilford, CT: Morris Book Publishing, 2011, 53–54.

Koikos, Jimmy, and Stacey Craig. In-person interview, September 29, 2014.

Koutroulakis, Gus. Interviewed by Amy Evans for the Southern Foodways Alliance, March 8, 2004.

Lee, Kristen. "I Come from a Family That Is Considered White." http://userwww.sfsu.edu/asu/Newsletter/nws04KLee2.html.

Lewis, James. In-person interview, November 3, 2014.

Matsos, Michael. Interviewed by Amy Evans for the Southern Foodways Alliance, October 3, 2006.

"Meet the Man Behind the Pies." Post Office Pies website. http://postofficepies.com/news/meet-the-man-behind-the-pies.

Morosini, Marco. Phone interview, January 8, 2014.

Newsome, Anna. Phone interview, December 2011.

Palmer, Rod. Phone interview, May 2012.

Papapietro, Mauricio. In-person interview, November 14, 2014.

Pasisis, Gus. In-person interview, October 9, 2014.

Pihakis, Nick. Phone interview, November 11, 2014.

Romero, Catherine. "Carole Griffin, Faces of Birmingham." Style Blueprint. http://styleblueprint.combirminghameveryday/carole-griffin-faces-birmingham.

Reis, George. Phone interview, May 15, 2013.

Reuters. "Zoe's Kitchen Aims to Raise $80.5 mln in IPO." March 10, 2014. http://www.reuters.comarticle/2014/03/10/zoeskitchen-ipo-idUSL3N0M74IS20140310.

Rucker, Ahmad. Phone interview, May 2013.

Russell, Mac. In-person interview, November 11, 2014.

Sarris, George. In-person interview, July 9, 2014.

Sissa, George. Interviewed by Amy Evans for the Southern Foodways Alliance, March 11, 2004.

Snow, David. Phone interview, May 2013.

Snyder, Andrea. Phone interviews, October 2011 and May 27, 2014.

Somershield, Brian. Phone interview, November 18, 2014.

Stitt, Frank. Phone and in-person interviews, February 2013 and September 16, 2014.

Stone, Deborah. Phone interview, May 2014.

Taylor, Joe Gray. *Eating, Drinking, and Visiting in the South: An Informal History*. Baton Rouge: Louisiana State University Press, 1982, 67–135.

Urban Standard. "Story." http://urbanstandard.net/about/story.

Watkins, Jim. Phone interview, June 2012.

Williams, Roy L. "Birmingham Restaurant Operator Michael Matsos Dies at 93." Al.com. http://blog.al.combusinessnews/2012/01/birmingham_restaurant_operator.html.

Wilson, Mike. Phone interview, November 18, 2014.

INDEX

T

U

V

W

Z

ABOUT THE AUTHOR

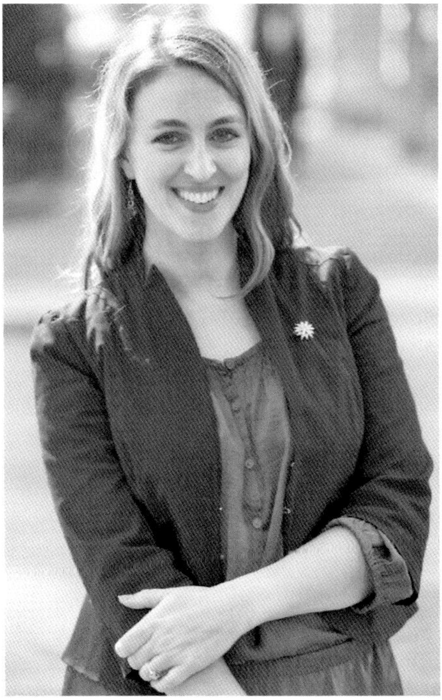

A proud Birmingham, Alabama native, Emily Brown has long been in on the secret that Birmingham is an incredible food town. When she's not writing about food, restaurants and purveyors for Birmingham Restaurant Week, she's out enjoying new culinary adventures, whether in one of the city's restaurants or from her own kitchen. Raised equally on a diet of storytelling and great southern food, Emily went on to gain her bachelor's degree in English from Birmingham-Southern College and her master's in creative writing from the University of North Carolina–Wilmington. This is her first book.